Burkhard Dretzke
Margaret I. Nester

STUDENT'S GUIDE TO FALSE FRIENDS, NEW FRIENDS AND OLD FRIENDS

Dr. Burkhard Dretzke and Margaret I. Nester, B. A.

Student's Guide to False Friends, New Friends and Old Friends

1. Auflage   Druck 6 5 4 3   Jahr 2000 99 98 97

Alle Drucke dieser Auflage können im Unterricht nebeneinander verwendet werden.

© 1990 Cornelsen Verlag, Berlin
Das Werk und seine Teile sind urheberrechtlich geschützt. Jede Verwertung in anderen als den gesetzlich zugelassenen Fällen bedarf deshalb der vorherigen schriftlichen Einwilligung des Verlages.

Druck: Fürst & Sohn, Berlin

ISBN 3-464-02423-7

Bestellnummer 24237

 gedruckt auf säurefreiem Papier, umweltschonend hergestellt aus chlorfrei gebleichten Faserstoffen

Inhalt

Einleitung	4
Abkürzungen und Symbole	5

Textteil

Text 1:	Mistakes	7
Text 2:	Sponsored Students	11
Text 3:	Violence on TV	15
Text 4:	The Open University	19
Text 5:	Keeping Out the Sun	25
Text 6:	Modern Museums	29
Text 7:	Traffic Jams – A Thing of the Past?	35
Text 8:	What a Weather!	39
Text 9:	Letter to a Friend	43
Text 10:	The Environmental Pollution Poses No Threat	47
Text 11:	The Modern European	51
Text 12:	Crime Does Pay!	55
Text 13:	Young People in the Eighties	61
Text 14:	School in West Germany	67
Text 15:	Communicating I	71
Text 16:	Communicating II	77

Lösungsteil

Texte 1 – 16	82
Korrekte Texte	114

Anhang 123

Einleitung

Das vorliegende Buch, das sich an Schülerinnen und Schüler, Studentinnen und Studenten sowie an Lehrerinnen und Lehrer wendet, versucht anhand von Texten auf mögliche Fehlerquellen beim Gebrauch und bei der Korrektur der englischen Sprache aufmerksam zu machen (Zielnorm: **Standard BE**). Als Hauptfehlerquelle beim Gebrauch des Englischen und teilweise bei der Identifizierung als Fehler erweisen sich oft sogenannte **false friends**. Diese „falschen Freunde" sind Fehler, die durch ihre orthographische, grammatische, phonetische und/oder besonders lexikalische Ähnlichkeit immer wieder inkorrekt verwendet werden, so daß sie schließlich zu „fossilierten Fehlern" werden.

Zweitens werden **old friends** behandelt, also *items*, die bei der Identifizierung von Fehlern manchmal Schwierigkeiten bereiten. „Alte Freunde" sind korrekt gelernte *items*, bei denen man aber unsicher ist, da sie durch die Strategie der Muttersprachenvermeidung und aufgrund der spezifischen Aufgabenstellung in diesem Buch so sehr in Zweifel gezogen werden, daß sie den Leserinnen und Lesern schließlich als falsch erscheinen. Der Hinweis auf alte Freunde soll dazu dienen, korrekt gelernte *items*, die in den vorliegenden Texten überwiegen, nicht zu vergessen.

Drittens werden **new friends** vorgestellt. Diese „neuen Freunde" beziehen sich auf Neuerungen in der englischen Sprache, die z.T. noch vor nicht allzu langer Zeit als falsch eingestuft wurden. Aufgrund der Entwicklungen innerhalb der englischen Sprache, aufgrund eines sich gewandelten Korrektheitsbegriffs und infolge einer anderen Einstellung der gebildeten Sprecher zum Sprachgebrauch sind diese Neuerungen in den Standardbereich aufgerückt. Insbesondere ist hier auf die sogenannten **divided usages** zu verweisen, die aus der Sicht der Linguisten gleichberechtigt neben den traditionellen *items* stehen.

Was die Neuerungen im Englischen betrifft, so sollen besonders die Arbeiten der *Survey of English Usage* erwähnt werden. Die Namen Quirk, Greenbaum, Leech und Svartvik (*Comprehensive Grammar of the English Language*. London: Longman 1985, später abgekürzt als *CGEL*) sowie auch Mittins sind hier zu nennen. Eine kurze zusammenfassende Darstellung über den heutigen Korrektheitsbegriff im Englischen sowie eine Bibliographie und eine Liste von Standardgrammatiken und -wörterbüchern befinden sich am Ende des Buches in einem Anhang.

Die vorliegenden Texte sind teilweise mit Fehlern versehen, teilweise sind sie aber auch völlig fehlerfrei. Damit die Leserinnen und Leser alle Texte kritisch lesen, wird auf die Texte, ob nun korrekt oder nicht, jeweils mit einem Warndreieck ⚠ hingewiesen. Dadurch, daß den Leserinnen und Lesern fehlerhafte Texte dargeboten werden, wird absichtlich eine pädagogische Häresie begangen, allerdings mit dem erklärten Ziel, endlich einmal den „fossilierten Fehlern" ernsthaft den Garaus zu machen. Denn es geht in diesem Buch um das bewußte Einüben der Fertigkeit, Fehler in Texten zu identifizieren, eine Fertigkeit, die ja bei jeder Korrektur als Selbstverständlichkeit vorausgesetzt wird. Am Ende des Buches finden die Benutzerinnen und Benutzer *alle* Texte völlig korrekt wiedergegeben. Für die Korrektheit sind die

Verfasserin und der Verfasser verantwortlich. Zu danken ist außerdem Dr. Jonathan Hope von der University of Newcastle-upon-Tyne, der die Texte mit englischen Studentinnen und Studenten durchgesehen hat. Schließlich sind wir Frau StAssin Christine Pilot und Herrn StD Torsten Kuhlmeyer für didaktisch-methodische Hinweise und Anregungen dankbar.

Das Buch besteht aus zwei Teilen. Im ersten Teil (Textteil) finden Sie die Texte mit der entsprechenden Fehlerkorrektur. An jeden dieser Texte schließen sich **Lernphasen** (Erklärungen und Fragen) und **Übungsphasen** (Übersetzungsaufgaben) an, die zur Erleichterung des Lernprozesses jeweils in zwei bis drei Abschnitte unterteilt sind. Im zweiten Teil (Lösungsteil) des Buches finden Sie die Lösungen zu den **Lernphasen** und **Übungsphasen** sowie die korrekten Texte. Die Texte wurden so ausgewählt, daß sie sich auch für eine inhaltliche Behandlung im Unterricht nutzen lassen. Das Buch kann sowohl im Selbststudium als auch im Unterricht an der Schule oder Hochschule Verwendung finden.

Abkürzungen und Symbole

AE	Amerikanisches Englisch
BE	Britisches Englisch
bes.	besonders
CGEL	*Comprehensive Grammar of the English Language*
fml.	formell
infml.	informell
intr.	intransitives Verb
jd.	jemand
jm.	jemandem
jn.	jemanden
pl.	Plural
sb.	somebody
sl.	Slang
sth.	something
tr.	transitives Verb
v.	Verb
*	inkorrektes Englisch in jedem Kontext
(*)	inkorrektes Englisch im vorliegenden Kontext
?	Korrektheit strittig

TEXTTEIL

Text 1

 Der folgende Text kann, muß aber nicht, typische Fehler deutschsprachiger Lernender enthalten. Lesen Sie den Text durch und markieren Sie die Stellen, die Ihrer Meinung nach falsch sind.

Mistakes

Teachers of English are ever faced with the difficult problem of what to correct in their student's written and oral performance. Since the English language is constantly changing and since the notion of correctness and standard is never hundred procent fixed, one must admit that the teachers' task is highly complicated. Furthermore, teachers are continually exposed to incorrect utterances from their students, so that ultimately teachers may have difficulties to recognize mistakes. Thus, teachers will either oversee mistakes or mark items as incorrect which are actually correct. One cannot blame the students, too, as it is of course typical for learners to do mistakes. Frankly spoken, it is highest time that somebody published a comprehensive guide to help teachers correct texts rightly.

Difficult areas in English where skills really do have to be developed are, for example, tense and aspect, proverbs, idioms and collocations. For example, can one talk about a "strong smoker"? Does the proverb "to carry owls to Athen" exist or should it be "to carry coal to Newcastle"? Can one say "I have been wanting to see this man for years"? And can an examination be "a piece of cake"? Hopefully, after working through this book, the reader will feel more competent to deal with such questions.

Haben Sie in dem Text Fehler gefunden? Zur Kontrolle bitte umblättern.

Fehlerkorrektur

Auf dieser Seite finden Sie die Liste der Fehler. Arbeiten Sie zunächst die Lern- und Übungsphasen durch und setzen Sie danach die korrekten Formen *im Sinnzusammenhang* in die dafür vorgesehenen Schreibräume unten ein.

1. (*) ever: _____

2. (*) student's performance: _____

3. (*) hundred: _____

4. * procent: _____

5. * have difficulties to recognize: _____
   _____

6. (*) oversee: _____

7. * cannot blame the students, too: _____
   _____

8. * typical for: _____

9. * do mistakes: _____

10. * frankly spoken: _____

11. * it is highest time: _____

12. * correct texts rightly: _____

13. * developped: _____

14. * a strong smoker: _____

15. * Athen: _____

16. * carry coal to Newcastle: _____
    _____

Lernphase 1

1. Schlagen Sie folgende Vokabeln in einem zweisprachigen Wörterbuch nach: *typisch für, Fehler machen, es ist höchste Zeit, Eulen nach Athen tragen, übersehen.*
2. *Immer* wird im (modernen) Englischen mit *always* übersetzt. In bestimmten Verbindungen steht auch *ever* wie beispielsweise *forever, whoever* und *whenever* (= immer wenn, jedesmal wenn).
3. Nach welchen Regeln erfolgt die Setzung des Apostrophs bei Substantiven im Englischen?
4. Welche Schwierigkeiten ergeben sich bei der Übersetzung von *hundert* und *tausend*?
5. Das englische Wort für *Prozent* kann auf zweierlei Weise geschrieben werden. Wie lauten die beiden korrekten Formen?
6. *Schwierigkeiten haben, etwas zu tun* heißt im Englischen *have difficulty (in) doing sth.*

Lernphase 2

1. Die Übersetzung von *auch nicht* ins Englische ist problematisch. Übersetzen Sie die folgenden Sätze ins Englische:
   a) Ich kann auch nicht schwimmen.
   b) Mein Freund auch nicht.
2. Sogenannte Partizipialkonstruktionen als Entsprechung zu kommentierenden Adverbien stehen im Englischen mit dem **Partizip Präsens** wie beispielsweise *frankly speaking, strictly speaking, roughly speaking* und *generally speaking*.
3. Welche Übersetzungen finden Sie in einem zweisprachigen Wörterbuch für *richtig*? Geben Sie Beispiele für typische Kollokationen.
4. Die korrekte Schreibung des **past** von *develop* ist *developed*. Welche Regel können Sie dafür geben?
5. Die korrekte Übersetzung von *starker Raucher* ist *heavy smoker*. Der Grund ist, daß in verschiedenen Sprachen Wörter unterschiedlich mit anderen Wörtern zusammenstehen bzw. kollokieren. Finden Sie drei typische Beispiele für Kollokationen im Englischen.
6. Bei der Benutzung von Sprichwörtern im Englischen ist allgemein Vorsicht geboten. Neben wörtlichen oder ähnlichen Entsprechungen gibt es Sprichwörter, welche völlig verschieden in den Sprachen sind. Beispiele:
   a) behave like a bull in a china shop = sich wie ein Elephant im Porzellanladen benehmen (ähnlich)
   b) It's all Greek to me. = Ich verstehe nur Bahnhof. (verschieden)
   c) That's not my cup of tea. = Das ist nicht meine Kragenweite. (verschieden)
7. Wie heißen die Städte Athen, Brüssel, Marseille und Neapel auf englisch?

Übungsphase 1

Übersetzen Sie ins Englische:
1. Sie hat ihn immer geliebt.
2. Die Aussprache der Schüler ist ziemlich schlecht.
3. Es ist typisch für ihn, daß er unhöflich ist.
4. Sie haben mehrere Rechtschreibefehler gemacht.
5. Ich kann auch nicht (kommen).
6. Nichtmuttersprachler haben oft Schwierigkeiten, das Englische korrekt auszusprechen.
7. Vom rechtlichen Standpunkt gesehen hat die Regierung keinen Fehler gemacht.
8. Offen gesagt ist er einfach nicht ehrlich.

Übungsphase 2

Übersetzen Sie ins Englische:
1. Es ist höchste Zeit, daß wir den Wagen verkaufen.
2. Sie hat den Satz nicht richtig ausgesprochen.
3. Wenn Sie Englisch richtig lernen wollen, sollten Sie nach England gehen.
4. Wie Geoffrey richtig bemerkte, sind die Geisteswissenschaften oft unterfinanziert.
5. Der Film wurde in einem Tag entwickelt.
6. Er ist ein starker Raucher.
7. Eulen nach Athen tragen
8. Ich bin kompetent genug, um englische Sprichwörter richtig zu benutzen.
9. Polen ist 90% katholisch.

Text 2

 Der folgende Text kann, muß aber nicht, typische Fehler deutschsprachiger Lernender enthalten. Lesen Sie den Text durch und markieren Sie die Stellen, die Ihrer Meinung nach falsch sind.

Sponsored Students

I have read an article recently about a new phenomen in British universities – the sponsored student. After leaving his gymnasium, John D. became a kind of stipend from a well-known firm of estate agents, enabling him to go to university. He was quoted as saying that a sponsored student certainly needs to be self-assured, as he must be prepared to display informations about his sponsoring firm in the form of slogans on T-shirts or other articles of clothing. John is good in geography and is studying property changes in England over the last 50 years. But he denied that being sponsored has effected his study in any way, although the most of his essays do end with a recommendation of his sponsoring firm. As the reader may have guessed, all what John wants to do after making his exams is to go to work for a certain firm of estate agents.

Haben Sie in dem Text Fehler gefunden? Zur Kontrolle bitte umblättern.

Text 2

Fehlerkorrektur

Auf dieser Seite finden Sie die Liste der Fehler. Arbeiten Sie zunächst die Lern- und Übungsphasen durch und setzen Sie danach die korrekten Formen *im Sinnzusammenhang* in die dafür vorgesehenen Schreibräume unten ein.

1. (*) I have read ... recently: _____
2. * phenomen: _____
3. (*) gymnasium: _____
4. (*) became: _____
5. (*) stipend: _____
6. * informations: _____
7. * good in geography: _____
8. (*) has effected: _____
9. (*) his study: _____
10. * the most of his essays: _____
11. * all what: _____
12. * making his exams: _____

Lernphase 1

1. Schlagen Sie folgende Vokabeln in einem zweisprachigen Wörterbuch nach: *Phänomen, Gymnasium* (BE und AE), *Stipendium*.
2. *Recently* kann sowohl „vor kurzem" als auch „in letzter Zeit" heißen, der Tempusgebrauch richtet sich je nach der Bedeutung. „Vor kurzem" wird mit dem **past**, „in letzter Zeit" mit dem **present perfect** konstruiert. Bilden Sie je zwei Beispielsätze.
3. Im Englischen gibt es für das deutsche *werden* mehrere Übersetzungsmöglichkeiten. Schlagen Sie in einer Grammatik unter dem Stichwort *werden* nach

und bilden Sie Sätze mit *to become, to come, to fall, to get, to go, to grow* und *to turn*.
4. **Bekommen** kann im Englischen mit *to get* (z.B. *What did you get for your birthday?*), *to receive* (z.B. *I have received hundreds of letters this week.*) und *to obtain* (z.B. *I obtained my degree at Cambridge.*) heißen. *To get* ist am wenigsten formell.
5. *Information* gehört im Englischen zu der Klasse der **uncountable nouns** wie auch *news*. Welche Konstruktionen sind mit *information* möglich?
6. Wie übersetzen Sie *gymnasium, stipend, his study* und *become* ins Deutsche?

Lernphase 2

1. Merke: *gymnasium* ist n i c h t *Gymnasium, become* ist n i c h t *bekommen* und *stipend* ist n i c h t *Stipendium*.
2. *Gut sein in Mathematik/Latein/Englisch* heißt im Englischen *to be good at mathematics/at Latin/at English*.
3. *Affect* und *effect* sind zwei leicht verwechselbare Verben. Schlagen Sie die Bedeutungen in einem zweisprachigen Wörterbuch nach und bilden Sie je zwei Beispielsätze mit Hilfe eines einsprachigen Wörterbuches.
4. Bilden Sie mit Hilfe eines einsprachigen Wörterbuchs zwei Sätze mit dem englischen Wort für *Studium*.
5. In welchem Kontext können Sie im Englischen *the most* sagen?
6. *Alles, was* heißt im obigen Kontext *all that* wie auch beispielsweise *All is well that ends well*. Vorzugsweise folgt ein *that* (dt. *was*) nach *all, everything, nothing* und *much*. Nach *something* kann entweder *that* oder *which* folgen. Im informellen Stil wird in der Objektform eine Konstruktion ohne Relativpronomen vorgezogen: *Everything you say is wrong*.
7. *Machen* heißt im Englischen oft *to make* oder *to do*. Meist entspricht dem deutschen *machen* das englische *to do* wie beispielsweise *to do homework/exercises*. *Ein Examen machen* heißt *to take an exam, to sit (for) an exam* (infml.) und auch *to do an exam* (infml.). Welche typischen Kollokationen gibt es mit *to do* und *to make?*

Übungsphase 1

Übersetzen Sie ins Englische:
1. In letzter Zeit habe ich viel gearbeitet.
2. Vor kurzem hat mich meine Freundin besucht.
3. Wie kann man diese Phänomene erklären?
4. Viele Eltern schicken ihre Kinder auf das Gymnasium.
5. Die Blätter werden gelb.
6. Die Milch ist sauer geworden.
7. Sie will Ärztin werden.

8. Sie wurde sehr böse mit ihm.
9. Viele Studenten können nur studieren, wenn sie ein Stipendium erhalten.
10. Die Informationen in der Zeitung stimmten nicht.

Übungsphase 2

Übersetzen Sie ins Englische:
1. Viele Schüler sind gut in Französisch.
2. Sie hat ihr Medizinstudium erfolgreich abgeschlossen.
3. Die meisten Leute können heutzutage lesen.
4. Ich glaube alles, was er gesagt hat.
5. Es ist nicht alles Gold, was glänzt.
6. Die Schüler machen ihre Abschlußprüfung immer im Sommer.
7. Sie ist besser in Physik als in Spanisch.
8. Mein Arbeitszimmer ist sehr klein.
9. Ich bin nicht überrascht, daß dein Studium darunter leidet.
10. Wird der Streik den Kohlepreis beeinflussen?

Text 3

 Der folgende Text kann, muß aber nicht, typische Fehler deutschsprachiger Lernender enthalten. Lesen Sie den Text durch und markieren Sie die Stellen, die Ihrer Meinung nach falsch sind.

Violence on TV

For principal reasons, it would of course be preferrable if people watched less TV as they do. But there is a so large choice of programs available that it is not surprising that the simple man on the street spends too much time at home, telecommander in hand and eyes glued to the screen. And, of course, the choice of viewing material has been greatly increased by the availability of video films. One of the most disturbing developments is the increase in the sales of video "nasties" – video films containing a particular high proportion of sex and violence. A recent parliamentary report showed that these videos are especially harmful for children, who do not remark that there is a difference between the life on the screen and the real life. Young sensible children have often nightmares and display increased aggression after watching such videos. We have even reached a stadium where older children challenge younger ones to watch videos which are really gruesome. We must fear that this trend will continue unless the government forms a comittee to undertake steps to have these video "nasties" banned.

Haben Sie in dem Text Fehler gefunden? Zur Kontrolle bitte umblättern.

Fehlerkorrektur

Auf dieser Seite finden Sie die Liste der Fehler. Arbeiten Sie zunächst die Lern- und Übungsphasen durch und setzen Sie danach die korrekten Formen *im Sinnzusammenhang* in die dafür vorgesehenen Schreibräume unten ein.

1. * for principal reasons: _____

2. * preferrable: _____

3. * less … as: _____

4. * a so large choice: _____

5. (*) programs: _____

6. (*) the simple man: _____

7. * the simple man on the street: _____
   _____

8. * telecommander: _____

9. * particular high proportion: _____
   _____

10. * harmful for: _____

11. (*) who do not remark: _____

12. * the life on the screen / * the real life: _____
    _____

13. (*) sensible children: _____

14. * have often nightmares: _____

15. (*) stadium: _____

16. (*) we must fear: _____

17. * comittee: _____

18. * undertake steps: _____

Lernphase 1

1. Schlagen Sie folgende Vokabeln in einem zweisprachigen Wörterbuch nach: *Fernbedienung, sensibel, Stadium*.
2. *Aus prinzipiellen Gründen* wird im Englischen häufig mit *on principle/for reasons of principle* übersetzt.
3. Wann werden Endkonsonanten bei zweisilbigen Wörtern im Englischen verdoppelt? Sind die folgenden Wörter *prefers, preferring, preferred* und *preferable* richtig geschrieben? Wie werden diese Wörter ausgesprochen?
4. Komparativisches *als* wie z.B. in *weniger als, glücklicher als* und *mehr als* wird mit *than* übersetzt (z.B. *less than, happier than, more than*). Die Aussprache von *than* im Satz ist immer [ðən].
5. *So* vor Adjektiven ist im Englischen *so*, vor Adjektiven + Substantiv *such (a)* oder *so ... (a)*. *Eine so große Auswahl* heißt also *such a big/large choice* oder *so big/large a choice*. Sofern der unbestimmte Artikel steht, wird dieser nachgestellt, also *such a*.
6. Wie erklären Sie die beiden unterschiedlichen Schreibungen *program* und *programme* im Englischen? Wie schreibt man *Telegramm* im Englischen?
7. Wie übersetzen Sie die englischen Wörter *sensible* und *stadium* ins Deutsche?

Lernphase 2

1. Merke: *sensible* ist n i c h t *sensibel, stadium* ist n i c h t *Stadium*.
2. Schwierigkeiten bereiten den Nichtmuttersprachlern immer wieder Kollokationen, da Wörter oft nur in Isolation gelernt werden. Wie übersetzen Sie *der einfache Mann auf der Straße, schädlich für* und *Schritte unternehmen* ins Englische?
3. Wann kann man im Englischen von *simple man/woman* sprechen?
4. Bei der Konstruktion von Adverb + Adjektiv + Nomen kommt es oft zu Fehlern, da Adverbien im Deutschen nicht markiert sind. *Ein besonders großes Fenster* und *ein äußerst schwieriges Buch* sind im Englischen *a particularly big window* und *an extremely difficult book*.
5. Welche Übersetzungen finden Sie für das deutsche Wort *bemerken* in einem zweisprachigen Wörterbuch? Bilden Sie je zwei Sätze mit Hilfe eines einsprachigen Wörterbuches.

6. *Das Leben* heißt im Englischen *life*. Welche anderen Wörter haben im Gegensatz zum Deutschen keinen Artikel? Merken Sie sich die folgenden Konstruktionen in diesem Zusammenhang: *nature, beautiful nature* und *the nature of these animals* (= *die Natur, die schöne Natur* und *die Natur dieser Tiere*).
7. *Children often have nightmares:* Adverbien stehen im Englischen normalerweise nie zwischen dem Verb und Objekt. Beispiele sind *I always read books at night* und *I sometimes go to the opera*. Diese Konstruktion sollte nicht verwechselt werden mit der Konstruktion to be + Adverb + Adjektiv wie in *I am always hungry* und *She is often cheerful*.
8. *Wir müssen befürchten* heißt im idiomatischen Englischen *it is (to be) feared* oder *we fear*.
9. Wie unterscheidet sich das deutsche Wort *Komitee* vom entsprechenden englischen Wort? Wie werden im Englischen die Wörter *Kommando, Kommerz* und *Komödie* geschrieben?

Übungsphase 1

Übersetzen Sie ins Englische:
1. Aus grundsätzlichen Gründen werde ich an dem Treffen nicht teilnehmen.
2. Die Rakete wird durch Fernbedienung gelenkt.
3. Ein allmählicher Wandel ist einem plötzlichen Wandel vorzuziehen.
4. Ich ziehe es vor, nicht darüber nachzudenken.
5. In diesem Jahr werde ich weniger Geld als im vorigen Jahr verdienen.
6. Ich hatte eine so große Menschenmenge nicht erwartet.
7. Ein solch schönes Wetter ist selten in England.
8. Der einfache Mann auf der Straße kann nicht verstehen, warum die Regierung keine Schritte unternimmt, um die Arbeitslosigkeit zu verringern.
9. Er ist ein einfacher Mann.

Übungsphase 2

Übersetzen Sie ins Englische:
1. Das alltägliche Leben kann oft langweilig sein.
2. Er hat oft seltsame Träume.
3. Sensible Menschen haben oft sehr gute Ideen.
4. Wir müssen befürchten, daß er in diesem Stadium scheitern könnte.
5. Das Fußballstadion war voller als sonst.
6. „Meine Schwester ist mir eine große Hilfe", bemerkte er.
7. Es ist schwierig, mit diesem Komitee zu arbeiten.
8. Ich habe sie nicht bemerkt.
9. Dieses Programm kann für Kinder schädlich sein.

Text 4

 Der folgende Text kann, muß aber nicht, typische Fehler deutschsprachiger Lernender enthalten. Lesen Sie den Text durch und markieren Sie die Stellen, die Ihrer Meinung nach falsch sind.

The Open University

In 1971, an education experiment began in Milton Keynes, England, which affected the life of thousands of people in Britain. This was the start of the Open University. The aim of the Open University is to provide degree courses (including promotions) for anyone, regardless of previous qualifications.

The Open University devotes itself almost entirely to teach by correspondence, although radio and television broadcasts are also part of the course. The university authorities work close with the BBC in planning the broadcasts. In fact, the TV screen is in some ways superior than a lecture room, allowing close-ups of experiments and providing glimpses of work in research centers, which might not otherwise be available for students. Students recieve weekly correspondence of programmed explanations and excercises and also book-lists complete with the names and adresses of bookshops where the books can be bought. The books are cheap, because publishers can mass-produce copies for the Open University which usually sell well and which sometimes become bestsellers. Science students can obtain material at home free of charge for carrying out experiments.

The personal contact between students and lecturers is established during summer courses lasting about two weeks at a normal university or college. Each student has also the opportunity all year round to visit a local study center, of which there are about two hundred all over the country. Here, he or she can work with other students under the guidance of a tutor. With this type of organization, the Open University needs a few buildings and little apparatus as it uses existing facilities in other universities during the summer vacation.

The Open University has consequently adhered to the principle of offering further education to people of all ages and walks of life, and they have eagerly grasped this opportunity. They range from workers who left the school at sixteen to professional people working for higher qualifications such as a BA, a MA or even a PhD. And now, as it nears its twentieth birthday, the standards and popularity of this institution appear to be as high as ever.

Haben Sie in dem Text Fehler gefunden? Zur Kontrolle bitte umblättern.

Fehlerkorrektur

Auf dieser Seite finden Sie die Liste der Fehler. Arbeiten Sie zunächst die Lern- und Übungsphasen durch und setzen Sie danach die korrekten Formen *im Sinnzusammenhang* in die dafür vorgesehenen Schreibräume unten ein.

1. * an education experiment: _____

   _____

2. * the life of thousands of people: _____

   _____

3. (*) promotions: _____
4. * devotes itself ... to teach: _____

   _____

5. * work close with the BBC: _____

   _____

6. * superior than: _____
7. (*) centers / (*) center: _____
8. (*) available for: _____
9. * recieve: _____
10. * excercises: _____
11. * adresses: _____
12. * bestsellers: _____
13. (*) the personal contact: _____
14. * each student has also the opportunity: _____

    _____

15. (*) a few buildings: _____
16. (*) consequently: _____
17. (*) who left the school: _____
18. * a MA: _____
19. (*) twentieth birthday: _____

Lernphase 1
1. Schlagen Sie folgende Vokabeln in einem zweisprachigen Wörterbuch nach: *Promotion* („Doktorprüfung") und *konsequent* (im Sinne von „beharrlich", „folgerichtig" bzw. „streng, hart").
2. Im Deutschen werden **Komposita** sehr oft aus zwei Nomen (N + N) gebildet wie beispielsweise *Medizin + Student = Medizinstudent, Erziehung + Reformen = Erziehungsreformen, Musik + Instrument = Musikinstrument* und *Arbeiter + Klasse = Arbeiterklasse*. Im Englischen werden diese deutschen Komposita oft durch eine Konstruktion Adjektiv (rein oder partizipial) + Nomen wiedergegeben. Die obigen Beispiele sind also mit *medical student, educational reforms, musical instrument* und *working class* zu übersetzen.
3. Bei der Konkretisierung von **Abstrakta** wird im Englischen bei Mehrzahlbedeutung in der Regel auch die pluralische Form benutzt. Beispiele sind *Some people have very easy lives* und *What a lot of people have terrible coughs!*
4. Welche verbale Konstruktion erfolgt nach *devote oneself to?* Bilden Sie zwei Beispielsätze.
5. Das englische Wort *close* ist in dieser Form sowohl ein Adjektiv als auch ein unmarkiertes Adverb. Als unmarkiertes Adverb kann *close* aber nur im räumlichen Sinn von „nah" verwendet werden wie z.B. in den Sätzen *Come close, The children followed close behind them* oder *They live quite close*. Ansonsten ist die Adverbform *closely*.
6. Normalerweise folgt nach einem **Komparativ** im Englischen ein *than* wie z.B. *better than, higher than* und *more beautiful than*. Nach *superior* und einigen anderen Komparativen lateinischen Ursprungs erfolgt ein *to*, es heißt also *superior to*. Listen Sie andere Beispiele auf.
7. Die amerikanische Schreibweise für BE *centre* ist *center*. Geben Sie drei weitere typische Unterschiede zwischen der AE- und BE-Schreibweise an.
8. Welche Präposition folgt *available* in der englischen Übersetzung des Satzes *Unsere fortgeschrittene Technologie ist allen Studenten zugänglich?*

Lernphase 2

1. Merke: *promotion* ist n i c h t *Promotion* („Doktorprüfung") und *consequent* ist n i c h t *konsequent* (im Sinne von „beharrlich", „folgerichtig" bzw. „streng, hart"). Welche Übersetzungsäquivalente finden Sie für *promotion* und *consequent(ly)?*
2. Wie lautet die korrekte Schreibweise von **recieve, *excercises, *adresses* und **bestsellers?* Welche Ursachen haben die falschen Schreibungen?
3. *Der persönliche Kontakt* heißt im Englischen in der Regel *personal contact*. Geben Sie eine Erklärung für die englische Konstruktion.
4. Geben Sie Regeln für die Stellung des Adverbs in den Sätzen *She is also intelligent* und *She also takes her car to school.*
5. Welcher Unterschied besteht zwischen *a few buildings* und *few buildings* bzw. *a few friends* und *few friends?*
6. Im BE gibt es Regeln bei der Verwendung des bestimmten Artikels im Zusammenhang mit Gebäuden. Sind diese Regeln immer mit denen im AE identisch? Welche Regeln und Ausnahmen finden sich im BE?
7. Es muß *an MA* heißen wie es auch *an MP* heißt. Dagegen heißt es *a European* und *a Union Jack*. Welche Regeln gibt es für diese Fälle?
8. *Geburtstag* und *Jahrestag* („jährlicher Gedenktag, Jubiläum") heißen im Englischen *birthday* und *anniversary*. Bilden Sie je drei Beispiele mit diesen Wörter unter Zuhilfenahme eines einsprachigen Wörterbuches.

Übungsphase 1

Übersetzen Sie ins Englische:
1. Der Reichtum einer Nation hängt oft von ihrem Bildungsniveau ab.
2. In dieser Region ist das Leben vieler Menschen durch die Luftverschmutzung gefährdet.
3. Es war auch sein Hochzeitstag.
4. Sie erhielt eine Menge Karten zu ihrem 18. Geburtstag.
5. Nachdem die Feiern zum 40. Jahrestag des Staates stattgefunden hatten, fegte eine friedvolle Revolution durch das Land.
6. In der Chemie ist die Promotion die Voraussetzung für eine erfolgreiche Karriere.
7. Sie nahm an einem Computerkurs teil, um ihre Aufstiegschancen zu verbessern.
8. Ich glaube, daß du konsequent (beharrlich) sein mußt, wenn du ein bestimmtes Ziel erreichen willst.
9. Er ist ein konsequenter Verfechter einer Strafgesetzreform.
10. Wir werden konsequent durchgreifen.
11. Sie hat ihr Leben der Hilfe von Blinden gewidmet.
12. In dieser Firma gibt es gute Beförderungsmöglichkeiten.
13. Die Bank lieh ihm kein Geld. Folglich ging er pleite.
14. Pro Jahr schreibt sie einen Bestseller.

Übungsphase 2

Übersetzen Sie ins Englische:
1. Komm nicht zu nah!
2. Sie untersuchte die Photos sehr genau.
3. Der Computer ist dem Buch weit überlegen.
4. Wo ist die Stadtmitte?
5. Wir wollen unsere Produkte für einen größeren Markt verfügbar machen.
6. Eine Liste der Bestseller erhalten Sie von Ihrem Buchhändler.
7. Sehen Sie sich die Übung 18 in Ihrem Buch an.
8. Ich kann die Adresse auf diesem Briefumschlag nicht lesen.
9. An jenem Punkt war der Funkkontakt abgebrochen.
10. In dieser Firma ist der persönliche Kontakt sehr wichtig.
11. An dieser Universität kann jeder Student einen B.A. und M.A. in Geschichte bekommen.
12. Die Stadt hat auch einige alte Gebäude.
13. Nur wenige Gebäude wurden im Krieg zerstört.
14. Ich haßte die Schule.

Text 5

 Der folgende Text kann, muß aber nicht, typische Fehler deutschsprachiger Lernender enthalten. Lesen Sie den Text durch und markieren Sie die Stellen, die Ihrer Meinung nach falsch sind.

Keeping Out the Sun

In these days, the "greenhouse effect" is a phrase with which we are all familiar. It is a result of the discharge of gases (from many and varied processes) which are causing the earth's temperature to raise. This would, in its turn, cause a world-wide change in climate resulting in a huge man made catastrophe.

A Swiss scientist has used his fantasy and come up with a plan, bordering on science fiction, to avoid the disruption of the climate caused by the greenhouse effect.

His plan is to place a series of mirrors in a special orbit to cast a shade over part of the earth. These mirrors would reflect a proportion of sunshine back into the space. His theory is, that the mirrors would compensate for a 2.5°C rise in the average global temperature, by reducing the amount of incoming sunshine by about 3.5 percent. His device would counteract greenhouse warming successfully. It is comparable to a sunshade of huge mirrors.

He claims that the scheme would cost the equivalent of the world's annual military expenditure, about four hundred billion English pounds. But, even using the latest lightweight materials to build the mirror satellites, it is estimated, that it would last twenty years to build them. Some people are of course likely to be sceptic – however, this is finally a high-tech solution to a problem requiring drastic measures.

Haben Sie in dem Text Fehler gefunden? Zur Kontrolle bitte umblättern.

Fehlerkorrektur

Auf dieser Seite finden Sie die Liste der Fehler. Arbeiten Sie zunächst die Lern- und Übungsphasen durch und setzen Sie danach die korrekten Formen *im Sinnzusammenhang* in die dafür vorgesehenen Schreibräume unten ein.

1. * in these days: _____

2. (*) to raise: _____

3. * has used his fantasy: _____

4. * to cast a shade over: _____

5. (*) the space: _____

6. * his theory is, that / * it is estimated, that: _____
   _____

7. * four hundred billion English pounds: _____
   _____

8. (*) it would last twenty years: _____
   _____

9. * to be sceptic: _____

10. (*) this is finally: _____

Lernphase 1

1. Schlagen Sie das Wort *Phantasie* in einem zweisprachigen Wörterbuch nach und bilden Sie mit den gefundenen Übersetzungen je zwei Sätze.
2. *Heutzutage, in diesen Tagen* heißt im Englischen *these days, damals, in jenen Tagen* dagegen *in those days*.
3. Zu einigen intransitiven Verben gibt es identische oder verwandte kausativ-transitiven Verben wie beispielsweise *fly – fly* oder *work – work* und *rise – raise*, *lie – lay* oder *fall – fell*. Bilden Sie für jedes Paar zwei Beispielsätze.

4. *Schatten* kann im Englischen sowohl *shade* als auch *shadow* heißen. Welche Bedeutungsunterschiede gibt es, und in welchem Kontext kann das jeweilige englische Wort benutzt werden?
5. *Space* im Sinne von Weltraum steht im Englischen ohne Artikel. *The space* wird häufig in der Bedeutung Zwischenraum benutzt.
6. Vor *that* (deutsch: *daß*) steht im Englischen n i e ein Komma!

Lernphase 2

1. *Einhundert englische Pfund* sind im Englischen entweder einfach *a hundred pounds* oder *a hundred pounds sterling*.
2. *Dauern* bzw. *andauern* kann im Englischen mit *to last* oder *to take* übersetzt werden. Erklären Sie den Bedeutungsunterschied und bilden Sie mit Hilfe eines einsprachigen Wörterbuchs je zwei Beispielsätze.
3. Was heißt *It would last twenty years*?
4. *Skeptisch* heißt im Englischen *sceptical* (AE meist *skeptical*). Es gibt aber auch die Form *sceptic* (AE meist *skeptic*). Was bedeutet die letztere Form?
5. Neben dem Wort *sceptic* existiert auch das Wort *septic*. Welcher Bedeutungsunterschied liegt vor und wie unterscheiden sich beide Wörter in der Aussprache?
6. In deutsch-englischen Wörterbüchern finden Sie unter der Eintragung für *schließlich* u.a. *eventually, finally, at last* und *after all*. Erklären Sie die Bedeutungsunterschiede und bilden Sie je zwei Beispielsätze.

Übungsphase 1

Übersetzen Sie ins Englische:
1. Heutzutage essen die Leute nicht soviel Fleisch wie früher.
2. Die Sonne geht im Osten auf.
3. Sie hob ihre Hand hoch.
4. Er lebt in einer Phantasiewelt.
5. Sie hat eine lebhafte Phantasie.
6. Mir ist es zu heiß in der Sonne. Gehen wir in den Schatten.
7. Als es dunkler wurde, wurden die Schatten länger.
8. Der Platz zwischen den beiden Autos war zu eng.
9. Der Satellit befand sich seit zwei Jahren im Weltraum.

Übungsphase 2

Übersetzen Sie ins Englische:
1. Sie sagte, daß sie früh kommen würde.
2. Ist es wahr, daß du heiratest?
3. Es dauert vierzig Stunden, um dieses Auto zu bauen.
4. Seine schlechte Laune wird nicht andauern.

5. Alle meinen, daß unsere Mannschaft gewinnt, aber ich bin skeptisch.
6. Der Skeptiker wird gegen diesen Plan argumentieren.
7. Ich weiß, daß er die Arbeit nicht beendet hat, aber schließlich ist er sehr beschäftigt.
8. Das Pfund ist schon wieder gefallen.

Text 6

 Der folgende Text kann, muß aber nicht, typische Fehler deutschsprachiger Lernender enthalten. Lesen Sie den Text durch und markieren Sie die Stellen, die Ihrer Meinung nach falsch sind.

Modern Museums

Traditional museums whose objects are displayed in glass cases seem to have lost their appeal and can no longer fulfill the expectations of today's public. It is apparent that less people are visiting the traditional type of museum. These days, the public wants to have "an experience" at the museum. This idea is not as new as one might think. It was Francis Bacon who paved the way for the modern museum by advocating the use of things rather than words for teaching children. The new British national curriculum for schools is right up to date in this respect by stressing the idea that everybody should have their own direct experience of objects and situations. It claims that "the rough feel of woven cloth, the smell of the stable or the taste of food smoked over an open fire can evoke images stronger than written or verbal explanations would ever do."
Consequently, the new museums look different to the old ones and will hopefully attract more visitors. In modern museums, the choice of experiences the visitor can participate in ranges from a Victorian sewer, a return to the womb, a television news production or the Fire of London to an earthquake. One can well imagine how he or she will feel in York when riding round the reconstructed streets of a Viking city, smelling herring and listening to Icelandic. Similarly, the Crusades Experience in Winchester, the Tales of Robin Hood in Nottingham and the Smugglers' Adventures in Hastings have followed in York's footsteps. The most sophisticated imitator is the Imperial War Museum's new Blitz Experience. It recreates a London air-raid shelter under attack and is highly realistic – the message is certainly conveyed loud and clear.
This trend to more realism has its supporters and critics. Supporters claim that it keeps the museums up to date with both subject matter and technology. Such displays are also easier for non-specialists to understand due to their down-to-earth presentation. Critics argue that such experiences cater for a passive TV generation and do not encourage the use of one's imagination. Some museums will no doubt follow this trend, others will refuse to even consider any changes and yet others simply do not need follow this new trend. As a spokesperson for the Tower of London explained: "Changes? No way! We have the authentic article. We are not into replications!"

Haben Sie in dem Text Fehler gefunden? Zur Kontrolle bitte umblättern.

Fehlerkorrektur

Der Text enthält k e i n e Fehler. Lesen Sie sich die Anmerkungen zu den einzelnen *items* durch.

1. museums whose objects
2. can no longer fulfill
3. today's public
4. less people are visiting
5. not as new as
6. everybody should have their own direct experience
7. verbal explanations
8. different to
9. will hopefully attract
10. one can well imagine how he or she will feel
11. York's footsteps
12. the Museum's new Blitz Experience
13. conveyed loud and clear
14. easier to understand due to their down-to-earth presentation
15. refuse to even consider
16. do not need follow
17. a spokesperson
18. no way

Lernphase 1

1. Das Relativpronomen *whose* kann sowohl bei Personen als auch bei Sachen stehen, daher ist *museums whose objects* korrekt: "… *whose* – unlike *who* and *whom* – can have personal reference … and also nonpersonal reference" (CGEL, 366).
2. Die Schreibweisen *fulfil* und *fulfill* (manchmal mit dem Zusatz AE) stehen gleichberechtigt nebeneinander. Aufgrund von Analogie (*fill, fulfilling*) setzt sich die letztere Schreibung auch im BE immer mehr durch.
3. Die Form *today's public* ist korrekt: "The genitive is further used with certain kinds of inanimate nouns … TEMPORAL NOUNS, eg: *the decade's* event, *this year's* sales, *a day's* work, *today's* paper" (CGEL, 324).
4. Bereits im Altenglischen konnte die Form *læs* mit dem Plural benutzt werden. Dieser Gebrauch verschwand im Laufe der Zeit, er setzt sich aber heutzutage wieder verstärkt durch: "There is a tendency to use *less* (instead of *fewer*) and *least* (instead of *fewest*) also with count nouns" (CGEL, 263).
5. In Analogie zu *as … as* hat sich die Form *not as … as* heutzutage gegenüber der alten Form *not so … as* als die gebräuchliche durchgesetzt. Beide Formen sind korrekt.

6. Neben der Form *everybody should have <u>their</u> own direct experience* finden sich im modernen Englischen auch weitere (korrekte) Formen wie *everybody should have <u>his</u> own direct experience* und in neuester Zeit *everybody should have <u>his or her</u> own direct experience:* "Difficulties of usage arise, however, because English has no sex-neutral 3rd person singular pronoun. Consequently, the plural pronoun *they* is often used informally in defiance of strict number concord, in coreference with the indefinite pronouns *everyone, everybody; someone, somebody; anyone, anybody; no one, nobody...* The use of the plural is also a means of avoiding the ... device of coordinating masculine and feminine" (CGEL, 342).
7. In den modernen englischen Wörterbüchern wird neben der traditionell als korrekt akzeptierten Form *oral explanations* auch *verbal explanations* aufgeführt.
8. Nach *different* können folgende Präpositionen stehen, die alle korrekt sind: *different from, different to* und *different than* (besonders AE). Bilden Sie je einen Beispielsatz.
9. Der Gebrauch von *hopefully* als Satzadverb (**disjunct**) setzt sich immer mehr im Englischen durch. Moderne englische Wörterbücher bemerken zu diesem Gebrauch, daß er jetzt im großen Maße akzeptiert wird (*Oxford Advanced Learner's Dictionary*, 1989: "its use ... is now widely accepted").

Lernphase 2

1. Bei dem Satz *one can well imagine how he or she will feel* liegt eine ähnliche Entwicklung wie bei dem Satz *everybody should have his/his or her/their own direct experience* vor. Die Entwicklung geht von der Folge *the visitor ... he* hin zu *the visitor ... he or she,* wenn dies gewünscht wird oder wünschenswert erscheint.
2. Die Formen *York's footsteps* und *Museum's new Blitz Experience* sind korrekt: "The genitive is further used with certain kinds of inanimate nouns ... GEOGRAPHICAL NAMES ..., eg: continents ... countries ... states ... cities and towns: *Hollywood's* studios, *London's* water supply ... 'LOCATIVE NOUNS' ..., eg: the *earth's* interior, the *world's* economy ... the *Club's* pianist ... the *hotel's* entrance" (CGEL, 324).
3. Neben der markierten Adverbform mit *-ly* bei *loud and clear* gibt es im Standardenglischen auch die unmarkierten Adverbformen: "... *speak loud and clear* is fully acceptable in standard English" (CGEL, 406). Die im Text stehende Form ist in Analogie zu *speak loud and clear* zu verstehen und ebenfalls korrekt.
4. Die Form *due to* ist ursprünglich eine Adjektivform und wurde dementsprechend zunächst nur mit *to be* konstruiert. Wegen der semantischen Nähe zu *because of* und *owing to* kommt es bei *due to* zu einer Funktionserweiterung, so daß Sätze wie *He arrived late due to the storm* von vielen gebildeten Sprechern als korrekt angesehen werden: "*Due to* is generally accepted as a complex preposition synonymous with *owing to*" (CGEL, 1123).
5. Die starre „Regel", die den sogenannten **split infinitive** absolut verdammt, existiert im modernen Englischen nicht mehr. Oft wird aus Gründen der

rhythmischen Eleganz und der Disambiguierung der **split infinitive** sogar vorgezogen. Der Satz *refuse to even consider* ist korrekt.
6. In dem Satz *do not need follow* wird erwartet, daß nach der *do*-Paraphrase die Form *to follow* folgt. Dennoch ist der obige Satz akzeptabel, da nach *dare* und *need* sogenannte Kontaminationen möglich sind: "Blends between the auxiliary construction and the main verb construction occur and seem to be widely acceptable" (CGEL, 138).
7. Die moderne Form *spokesperson* versucht, eventuellen sexistischen Vorurteilen zu begegnen, und kann die Form *spokesman* oder auch *spokeswoman* ersetzen. Vor allem in offiziellen und formellen Kontexten wird die Form mit *-person* oft vorgezogen. So wird z.B. aus *one man, one vote* heutzutage *one person, one vote*.
8. Der emotionell gefärbte Ausdruck *no way* ist im informellen Bereich völlig korrekt und wird wegen seiner Kürze dort immer häufiger verwendet.

Text 6 kann aufgrund der obigen Ausführungen als völlig korrekt *(acceptable)* angesehen werden. Nur wenn ein formelles, geschriebenes Englisch gefordert ist, sind einige *items* stilistisch unangebracht *(inappropriate)*, nicht aber inkorrekt *(unacceptable)*.

Übersetzen Sie die folgenden Sätze ins Englische. Verwenden Sie formelle und informelle Formen, gebräuchliche und weniger gebräuchliche Formen, Varianten sowie BE und AE, soweit dies möglich ist.

Übungsphase 1

1. Es ist das Haus, dessen Dach beschädigt ist.
2. Eine Krankenschwester hat viele Aufgaben zu erfüllen.
3. Die heutige Öffentlichkeit interessiert sich nicht für diese Frage.
4. Sie haben dieses Mal weniger Fehler als das letzte Mal gemacht.
5. Jane ist nicht so groß wie Margaret.
6. Jeder glaubt, er habe ein Recht zu bleiben.
7. Ich werde meine Ansichten den Mitgliedern des Komitees mündlich mitteilen.
8. Mary und Joan sind voneinander ziemlich verschieden.
9. Die Studentinnen und Studenten dieses Proseminars werden hoffentlich den Abschlußtest bestehen.
10. Manch ein Student erkennt nicht, daß er für Prüfungen hart arbeiten muß. Manch ein/e Student/in erkennt nicht, daß er oder sie für Prüfungen hart arbeiten muß.

Übungsphase 2

1. Berlins berühmteste Baudenkmäler liegen in der Mitte der Stadt.
2. Die Schätze des Museums können zum ersten Mal besichtigt werden.

3. Sie sprach laut und deutlich.
4. Wegen des Schnees verpaßten sie die Fähre.
5. Ich will schnell zu Boots fahren, um mein Rezept abzuholen.
6. Ich wage nicht zu widersprechen.
7. Sie brauchen ihre Ratschläge nicht zu befolgen.
8. Die Sprecherin/der Sprecher der Gruppe war äußerst intelligent.
9. Auf keinen Fall will ich Ihr Angebot annehmen.

Text 7

 Der folgende Text kann, muß aber nicht, typische Fehler deutschsprachiger Lernender enthalten. Lesen Sie den Text durch und markieren Sie die Stellen, die Ihrer Meinung nach falsch sind.

Traffic Jams – A Thing of the Past?

Los Angeles boasts of the three busiest roads of the world and consequently the worst traffic jams. Planners reckon that in the next twenty years the number of daily car journeys will rise by fourty percent, and the average speed on freeways will be halfed. There are many possible solutions for this problem. The car lobby would like money to be spent for new roads. Local authorities in Los Angeles would like to repeat the experience of the 1984 Olympics, when an increase in the number of bus journeys and staggered journey times kept Los Angeles free of traffic jams for two weeks. Rail enthusiasts are pinning their hope on a projected new light railway. But the most promising solutions rely on new technique – research is being done in three main fields.

Firstly, streets are being equiped with road sensors which monitor traffic flow and are linked to central computers. These instantly adjust traffic lights to control the traffic. A second system aims at placing computers in cars, giving drivers up to the minute advices about road conditions ahead (for example accidents or jams), thus enabling them to take alternative routes. Cars could also be fitted with radar which relays signals to a computer situated in the car and prevents collisions by automatically breaking the car. Eventually, one of the safety measures might include a device whereby a driver who has had a couple of drinks too much will automatically be prevented to drive his or her car.

The overall aim is to automate driving – similar to the way modern aeroplanes function – taking much of the control of driving out of the driver's hand. A further problem may of course be providing parking spaces for all the extra cars which this system allows to use the city streets!

Haben Sie in dem Text Fehler gefunden? Zur Kontrolle bitte umblättern.

Fehlerkorrektur

Auf dieser Seite finden Sie die Liste der Fehler. Arbeiten Sie zunächst die Lern- und Übungsphasen durch und setzen Sie danach die korrekten Formen *im Sinnzusammenhang* in die dafür vorgesehenen Schreibräume unten ein.

1. (*) boasts of: _____

2. * busiest roads of the world: _____

_____

3. * fourty: _____

4. * will be halfed: _____

5. * solutions for this problem: _____

_____

6. * to be spent for: _____

7. * enthusiasts are pinning their hope: _____

_____

8. (*) new technique: _____

9. * being equiped: _____

10. * advices: _____

11. * advices about: _____

12. (*) breaking the car: _____

13. * a couple of drinks too much: _____

_____

14. * prevented to drive: _____

15. (*) out of the driver's hand: _____

Lernphase 1

1. Schlagen Sie das Wort *Technik* in einem zweisprachigen Wörterbuch nach und bilden Sie mit den Übersetzungsäquivalenten je zwei Beispielsätze.
2. In Wörterbüchern finden Sie für das Verb *boast* sowohl die Konstruktion *boast sth.* als auch *boast of/about*. Erklären Sie den Unterschied.
3. Im Englischen gibt es verschiedene Kollokationen mit *world*. Nennen Sie vier häufige Verbindungen. Welche Regel finden Sie für die Konstruktion *in the world?*
4. Wie werden *vier, vierzehn* und *vierzig* im Englischen geschrieben?
5. Wie bei der Pluralbildung einiger Substantive ein finales *-f* zu *-v(es)* wird (vgl. *life – lives, shelf – shelves, half – halves*), so schreibt man die Verbform ebenfalls mit *-v* (*halve, halving, halved*).
6. Präpositionsfehler sind sehr häufig bei Lernenden anzutreffen. So werden immer wieder Fehler bei der Übersetzung der Präposition *für* gemacht. Wie heißen im Englischen *typisch für, charakteristisch für, gelten für* und *ausgeben für* sowie *Lösung für, Symbol für, Beispiel für, Zeichen für, Grund für* und *Beweis für?*

Lernphase 2

1. Als idiomatischer/metaphorischer Ausdruck heißt es *pin one's hopes on*. In diesem Falle muß also der Plural stehen. Allerdings gibt es auch gegenteilige Beispiele (s. CGEL, 768).
2. Welche Schreibregel gibt es für einfache, betonte Endkonsonanten bei vokalisch anlautenden Endungen? Gibt es Ausnahmen zu dieser Regel? Bilden Sie die Vergangenheitsform von *prefer, regret, develop, travel, worship* und *panic*.
3. *Ratschlag* bzw. *Rat* und *Ratschläge* heißt im Englischen *advice*. Wie übersetzt man *ein Ratschlag, wie man etwas macht?*
4. Erläutern Sie den Unterschied zwischen *brake the car* und *break the car*.
5. Im Englischen ist man bei der Verwendung von *zuviel* genauer als im Deutschen, man übersetzt *zuviel* entweder mit *too much* oder mit *too many*. Im obigen Satz muß es *too many* heißen. Finden Sie zwei weitere Sätze, in denen *zuviel* mit *too many* übersetzt wird.
6. *Jemanden daran hindern, etwas zu tun* wird im Englischen mit *prevent sb. (from) doing sth.* übersetzt. Dabei gehört die Konstruktion ohne *from* eher dem informellen Stil an. Bilden Sie mit der englischen Form *prevent sb. (from) doing sth.* zwei Sätze.
7. Erklären Sie den Unterschied zwischen *out of the driver's hand* und *out of the driver's hands*. Welche Konstruktion ist im obigen Kontext angemessener?

Übungsphase 1

Übersetzen Sie ins Englische:
1. Unsere Straße kann sich rühmen, die ältesten Häuser der Stadt zu haben.
2. Er prahlt aber auch immer mit seinen Kindern.
3. Sie ist die reichste Frau der Welt.
4. Im nächsten Jahr werde ich vierundvierzig.
5. Sie versuchte, die Kosten des Projekts zu halbieren.
6. Es gibt keine einfachen Lösungen für das Problem der Arbeitslosigkeit.
7. Wofür hast du das Geld ausgegeben?
8. Sie setzten ihre Hoffnung auf die neue Regierung.
9. Wenn Sie malen lernen wollen, schlage ich vor, daß Sie Turners Technik studieren.
10. Diese Druckerei verwendet die modernste Technik.

Übungsphase 2

Übersetzen Sie ins Englische:
1. Das ist eines der gut ausgestatteten Krankenhäuser.
2. Kann ich Ihnen einen Ratschlag geben?
3. Sie wollen Ratschläge, wie sie die Situation meistern können.
4. Seien Sie vorsichtig beim Bremsen! Sie könnten den Motor abwürgen.
5. Vater zum Sohn: „Mach das Auto nicht kaputt!"
6. Er hatte ein Glas zuviel getrunken.
7. Sie wurden daran gehindert, auf der Straße zu demonstrieren.
8. Sie nahm das Kind bei der Hand.
9. Die Liebenden standen händehaltend vor dem Geschäft.

Text 8

 Der folgende Text kann, muß aber nicht, typische Fehler deutschsprachiger Lernender enthalten. Lesen Sie den Text durch und markieren Sie die Stellen, die Ihrer Meinung nach falsch sind.

What a Weather!

Humans first set foot on Britain more than half a million years ago. The surprising fact is that ancient Britons appear to have stayed on only when the weather was inclement. Britons apparently clung to their shores just so that they could go on to complain about the weather! Archaeologists have remarked that when the climate became warm and food in the form of bison and mammoth roamed the land, ancient Britons seem to have vanished – as evidenced by a stark lack of remains from these times.

The climate has regularly swung between periods of very hot and cold weather, from ice ages to heatwaves. In between these extremes, the country was covered with tundra and wet mists. We would find this rather inhospitable as we are currently going through a warm period and are used to live in much better conditions. We also learn of archaeologists that Britain was nevertheless inhabitable with its tundra and mist and that ancient Britons seem to have thrived on it, since nearly all ancient sites in Britain date from these cool periods. Obviously, such a weather represented no threat for ancient Britons. For example, a huge mammoth graveyard uncovered near Ipswich indicates a spot where dozens animals died. Bearing in mind that mammoths roamed the land in warm conditions, they should have provided food for scavenging humans, but flints – the only sure proof for ancient humans' presence – are totally missing. In so far as our information about this period is correct, there is strong reason to believe that there were simply no humans around to take advantage from this opportunity.

Various explanations, the most of them not very satisfactory, have been put forward, but the only certain conclusion seems to be that ancient Britons appear to have had a strange urge to hang about in the cold and rain!

Haben Sie in dem Text Fehler gefunden? Zur Kontrolle bitte umblättern.

Fehlerkorrektur

Auf dieser Seite finden Sie die Liste der Fehler. Arbeiten Sie zunächst die Lern- und Übungsphasen durch und setzen Sie danach die korrekten Formen *im Sinnzusammenhang* in die dafür vorgesehenen Schreibräume unten ein.

1. * what a weather / * such a weather: _____

2. (*) set foot on: _____

3. (*) go on to complain: _____

4. (*) have remarked: _____

5. * are used to live: _____

6. (*) learn of archaeologists: _____

7. * threat for ancient Britons: _____

8. * dozens animals: _____

9. (*) proof for: _____

10. * to take advantage from: _____

11. * the most of them: _____

Lernphase 1

1. Das englische Wort *weather* kann nicht mit dem unbestimmten Artikel gebraucht werden. Man sagt also *What beautiful weather!* Andererseits kann es aber im Plural stehen: "... some nouns, like *weather*, are neither count (**a weather*) nor noncount (**a lot of weather*), but these nouns share features belonging to both classes. Noncount noun features include the premodified structures *a lot of good weather, some bad weather, what lovely weather.* On the other hand, count noun features include the plural *go out in all weathers, in the worst of weathers*" (CGEL, 252).
2. Man sagt *set foot on British soil* und *set foot in Britain.* Suchen Sie in einem einsprachigen Wörterbuch nach zwei weiteren Konstruktionen.
3. Vergleichen Sie die beiden Sätze *The guest became very angry and went on to complain at length about the hotel* und *The guest became very angry and went on complaining for hours about the food in the hotel.* Wie erklären Sie den Unterschied der Konstruktion nach *went on?*
4. Das deutsche Wort *bemerken* kann u.a. mit *remark, notice* oder *realize* übersetzt werden. Wie unterscheiden sich die drei Wörter (s. Text 3, Lernphase 2, Nummer 5)?
5. Wie werden *they used to, they are used to* und *they get used to* konstruiert, und welche Bedeutungsunterschiede liegen vor? Bilden Sie je einen Beispielsatz.
6. Wie übersetzen Sie *learn of/about* und *learn from* ins Deutsche? Bilden Sie je zwei Beispielsätze.

Lernphase 2

1. Sie finden sowohl *threat of* als auch *threat to* im Englischen. Erklären Sie den Unterschied und bilden Sie je zwei Beispielsätze.
2. Merke: *dozens of glasses, hundreds of spectators, thousands of people* und *millions of inhabitants.*
3. Welche Bedeutungen hat *proof?* Was heißt *Beweis(e) für* im Englischen?
4. Wie übersetzen Sie *etwas ausnutzen* ins Englische? Bilden Sie zwei Beispielsätze.
5. Der deutschen Konstruktion *die meisten* + Nomen entspricht im Englischen *most* + Nomen. In diesem Fall steht im Englischen kein bestimmter Artikel (s. Text 2, Lernphase 2, Nummer 5)!

Übungsphase 1

Übersetzen Sie ins Englische:
1. Was für ein scheußliches Wetter!
2. Sie waren die ersten, die die Insel betraten.
3. Sie waren die ersten, die aus der Türe traten.
4. Sie waren die ersten Europäer, die Amerika betraten.
5. Trotz der guten Wirtschaftslage beklagten sie sich weiterhin.

6. Sie unterbrach ihre Rede und fuhr dann fort, indem sie sich über die Nachlässigkeit der Industrie beschwerte (und dann/danach beklagte sie sich über die Nachlässigkeit der Industrie).
7. „Eine gute Idee", bemerkte sie.
8. Sie bemerkte, daß sie ihre Schlüssel vergessen hatte.
9. Wir wohnten früher in London.
10. Sie sind es gewohnt, Gäste zu haben.
11. Wir gewöhnen uns daran, Gäste zu haben.

Übungsphase 2

Übersetzen Sie ins Englische:
1. Er scheint nie aus seinen Fehlern zu lernen.
2. Wir erfuhren von der Hochzeit unserer Tochter auf dem Weg nach Paris.
3. Die Luftverschmutzung ist eine Bedrohung für die ganze Menschheit.
4. Es drohte zu regnen.
5. Es gab Dutzende Versuche, die Schule zu reformieren.
6. Haben Sie einen Beweis für seine Schuld?
7. Ich habe gestern die Korrekturfahnen erhalten.
8. Sie sollten das schöne Wetter ausnutzen.
9. Die meisten Leute nehmen ihren Urlaub im Sommer.

Text 9

 Der folgende Text kann, muß aber nicht, typische Fehler deutschsprachiger Lernender enthalten. Lesen Sie den Text durch und markieren Sie die Stellen, die Ihrer Meinung nach falsch sind.

Letter to a Friend

... So, after sitting my A levels, I decided to study at London University – you know I always wanted to be a teacher – my life's aim and all that! Well, the first week in London was quite awful. I caught a cold straight after I arrived. Fortunately, it wasn't flu, but I still went to the chemist for some medicine and thought I better stay in bed for a while. But I soon got over it and got around to exploring. I found my way around the university buildings, found out about the lecture rooms, and had a good look at the students' union. They certainly provide everything you need, including banking facilities, so I opened an account at Barclays.

When I had a bit of time, I went shopping – even went to Harrods. Of course, clotheswise there was a lot of choice, but Harrods were just too expensive.

Anyway, I got through the first year and was dreading the exams, but I had to face them now. Everybody has their off days which always seem to fall on exam days! But the ordeal was soon over and the results were published three weeks later. Very nervous, everybody rushed to the main building to see how they had done. I tried to find my name and it took me a half hour to realise I was looking at the wrong list! But in the end I found my name and went home happy and relieved, looking forward to a several weeks vacation.

I know you haven't quite decided what you want to do yet, but if I was you I'd take the plunge and apply for university – you could do worse!

Haben Sie in dem Text Fehler gefunden? Zur Kontrolle bitte umblättern.

Fehlerkorrektur

Der Text enthält k e i n e Fehler. Lesen Sie sich die Anmerkungen zu den einzelnen *items* durch.

1. my life's aim
2. after I arrived
3. it wasn't
4. it wasn't flu
5. went to the chemist
6. I better stay
7. at Barclays
8. Harrods
9. clotheswise
10. Harrods were
11. I had to face them now
12. very nervous, everybody rushed
13. a half hour
14. went home happy
15. a several weeks vacation
16. if I was you

Lernphase 1

1. Neben *my aim in life* ist *my life's aim* auch möglich: "The genitive is further used with certain kinds of inanimate nouns ... NOUNS 'OF SPECIAL RELEVANCE TO HUMAN ACTIVITY', eg: the brain's total weight, the mind's development, the body's needs, my life's aim" (CGEL, 324).
2. Neben *after I had arrived* kann auch die Form *after I arrived* benutzt werden: "In some cases, particularly in a clause introduced by *after,* the two constructions can be more or less interchangeable..." (CGEL, 196).
3. Die Formen *it was not* und *it wasn't* sind beide korrekt: "Contractions are phonologically reduced or simplified forms which are institutionalized in both speech and writing ... the contraction is favoured in informal style" (CGEL, 123).
4. Beide Formen, *the flu* und *flu,* sind gebräuchlich: "The zero article is normally used for illnesses, eg: *anaemia, appendicitis, diabetes, influenza, pneumonia*. But *the* is often used, in a more traditional style of speech, for some well-known infectious diseases: *(the) flu, (the) measles, (the) mumps, (the) chicken pox ...*" (CGEL, 279).
5. Die traditionelle Form ist *went to the chemist's,* während die neuere Form *went to the chemist* ist: "The 'local genitive' is used ... (iii) For places where business is conducted: *the barber's, the hairdresser's ... the chemist's ...* . The *'s* is often dropped: at/to the chemist" (CGEL, 330).

6. Neben der Form *I had better stay* existiert auch die Form *I better stay:* "In informal speech, the first word of ... had better is often completely elided .... This reduction is represented in very informal written style ... by the omission of ...'d" (CGEL, 142).
7. *At Barclays, to Harrods* und *Harrods were* werden im modernen Englisch als korrekt akzeptiert: "With large businesses, their complexity and in some sense plurality causes reinterpretation of the *-s* ending as a plural rather than genitive inflection (*Barclays, Harrods, Selfridges, Woolworths*). The genitive meaning – if it survives – is expressed by moving the apostrophe: at Macys'. This uncertainty over the status of the -s ending is matched by a vacillation in concord, reflecting the conflict between plurality and the idea of a business as a collective unity: *Harrods is/are* very good for clothes" (CGEL, 330).

Lernphase 2

1. Wie sich im Deutschen besonders unter der jungen Generation Wortbildungen mit *-mäßig* verstärkt durchsetzen (*wettermäßig, geldmäßig*), so findet sich im Englischen eine ähnliche Tendenz bei Wortbildungen mit *-wise:* "Viewpoint subjuncts can also be formed from nouns by the addition of the suffix *-wise* (especially in AE), though these are considered informal:
Program-wise, the new thing on TV last night was the first part of a new Galsworthy dramatization.
Weatherwise, we are going to have a bad time this winter" (CGEL, 568).
Die Form *clotheswise* (auch *clothes-wise*) ist somit korrekt.
2. *I had to face them now* ist ebenfalls korrekt: "Note that *now* can also be used with reference to the past: They had been courting for two years and he *now* felt she knew his worst faults" (CGEL, 530).
3. Die Konstruktion *very nervous, everybody rushed ...* ist korrekt: "Adjectives can function as the sole realization of a verbless clause ... or as the head of an adjective phrase realizing the clause: ... *Rather nervous,* the man opened the letter" (CGEL, 424-425).
4. Die Form *a half hour* ist korrekt, allerdings ist die Form *half an hour* im BE weitaus gebräuchlicher: "*Half,* normally a predeterminer, as in *half a loaf, half an hour ...,* also occurs occasionally as a postdeterminer: *a half loaf, a half hour*" (CGEL, 388).
5. Die Adjektivform in dem Satz *went home happy* ist korrekt. Der Satz kann mit *I was happy when I went home* paraphrasiert werden. In diesem Falle drückt das Adjektiv einen Zustand aus, es bleibt daher unveränderlich (s. CGEL, 1171 ff.). Die Adverbform *happily* würde die Handlung selbst modifizieren.
6. Neben der hier aufgeführten Form *a several weeks vacation* gibt es noch drei weitere korrekte Formen: "... in quantitative expressions of the following type there is possible variation ... : *a ten day absence, a ten-day absence ... a ten days absence ... a ten days' absence*" (CGEL, 1333).

7. Beide Formen, *if I was you* und *if I were you,* sind korrekt: "The were- subjunctive ... is hypothetical or unreal in meaning, being used in adverbial clauses introduced by such conjunctions as *if, as if, as though*... This subjunctive is limited to the one form *were*... The indicative form *was* is substituted in less formal style: If I *were/was* rich, I would buy you anything you wanted... The idiom *if I ... you* by convention usually contains the subjunctive *were,* though *was* also occurs frequently" (CGEL, 158, 1094).

Text 9 kann aufgrund der obigen Ausführungen als völlig korrekt *(acceptable)* eingestuft werden, da es sich um ein informelles, geschriebenes Schriftstück („Brief an eine Freundin") handelt. Nur wenn ein formelles, geschriebenes Englisch gefordert ist, sind einige *items* stilistisch unangebracht *(inappropriate),* nicht aber inkorrekt *(unacceptable).*

Übersetzen Sie die folgenden Sätze ins Englische. Verwenden Sie formelle und informelle Formen, gebräuchliche und weniger gebräuchliche Formen, Varianten sowie BE und AE, soweit dies möglich ist.

Übungsphase 1

1. Mein Lebensziel ist es, erfolgreich zu sein.
2. Ich aß zu Mittag, nachdem Jane vom Einkaufen zurückgekommen war.
3. Es war nicht zu heiß.
4. Wir hatten alle Grippe.
5. Ich mußte noch zum Friseur gehen.
6. Es wäre besser, wenn du zu Hause bliebest.
7. Ich habe ein Konto bei der Barclaybank.

Übungsphase 2

1. Was das Wetter betraf, so war der letzte Sommer phantastisch.
2. Harrods hat dieses Jahr mehr Porzellan verkauft als im letzten Jahr.
3. Sie fühlte jetzt, daß sie etwas tun mußte.
4. Ich brauchte eine halbe Stunde, um zum Bahnhof zu kommen.
5. Sie hatte ihr Examen bestanden und ging glücklich nach Hause.
6. Die Frau betrat das Hotel ziemlich selbstbewußt.
7. Ich freue mich auf einen fünftägigen Aufenthalt in Berlin.
8. Wenn ich ein Schauspieler wäre, würde ich nur ernste Rollen spielen.

Text 10

 Der folgende Text kann, muß aber nicht, typische Fehler deutschsprachiger Lernender enthalten. Lesen Sie den Text durch und markieren Sie die Stellen, die Ihrer Meinung nach falsch sind.

The Environmental Pollution Poses No Threat

If ecological experts are to be believed, the future of the planet Earth looks grimly indeed. We are slowly extinguishing the natural environment with loops of concrete across the countryside carrying cars belching toxic fumes, with concrete tower blocks excluding all sunlight, and with fabrics and power stations doing their best to choke us to death. And we are poisoning the soil, rivers, the air – the list is inexhaustible. We can already imagine how the earth will look like if we do not put a stop to the pollution immediately.

Faced with this gloomy prospect, the efforts of societies to save an only tree, or restore an ancient building seem futile and irrelevant. So why keep on to worry about environmental friendly behaviour? Why try to put off the inevitable? Picking up a sweet paper to put it into a litter bin or switching off the motor of a car at traffic lights seems comicly absurd.

If we consider the fact that earlier creatures coped with changes in the environment and adapted – why can't we? The optimist in us stirs. All the old guilty feelings associated with, for example, not doing enough exercise to keep us fit, fall away. No more jogging, walking, or press-ups. The "New Human Beings" are pear-shaped, soft, and self-complacent. They can eat fattening foods without any fears. The slavery of cleaning teeth is over. Nourished of the sugary delights of the supermarket in soft or liquid form, they will no longer need their meat-eating teeth, which will simply fall out. They will no more be allergical against bad air, but will be able to inhale poisonous fumes, knowing they are evolving a lung to flourish on them. They can take up lodgings underneath the flight path to an airport, knowing that their ear-drums are evolving to cope with the thunder of landing planes.

Their families will learn to picnic in underpasses and on fly-overs (fields will have disappeared), eating pre-packed food to the roar of traffic and amplified music. As for human language, its loss will not be too tragical, since post-verbal communication will be in the form of grunts and grimaces. So, prepare for mutation. It's later than you think.

Haben Sie in dem Text Fehler gefunden? Zur Kontrolle bitte umblättern.

Fehlerkorrektur

Auf dieser Seite finden Sie die Liste der Fehler. Arbeiten Sie zunächst die Lern- und Übungsphasen durch und setzen Sie danach die korrekten Formen *im Sinnzusammenhang* in die dafür vorgesehenen Schreibräume unten ein.

1. * the environmental pollution / * stop the pollution: _____

2. (*) looks grimly: _____
3. (*) fabrics: _____
4. * how the earth will look like: _____

5. * an only tree: _____
6. * keep on to worry: _____
7. * environmental friendly: _____
8. (*) to put it into: _____
9. * the motor of a car: _____
10. * comicly: _____
11. (*) to keep us fit: _____
12. * nourished of: _____
13. * they will no more be: _____
14. * allergical against: _____
15. * they are evolving a lung: _____

16. * tragical: _____

Lernphase 1

1. Schlagen Sie folgende Vokabeln in einem zweisprachigen Wörterbuch nach: *Fabrik, Motor, Lunge*. Bilden Sie je einen Beispielsatz mit den gefundenen Übersetzungsäquivalenten.
2. *Pollution* gehört zu den abstrakten Begriffen, die nicht mit dem bestimmten Artikel stehen. Es heißt daher *pollution* und *environmental pollution*.
3. Zu den "verbindenden Verben" (Kopulaverben) gehören neben beispielsweise *be, seem, keep* und *become* auch die Klasse der Verben, die eine sinnlich wahrnehmbare Eigenschaft ausdrücken: *look, smell, feel, sound* und *taste*. Diese haben ein Adjektiv als Subjektkomplement.
Beispiele:
It tastes sour/horrible/nice. It feels hard/soft/dry.
Merke aber: Die Verben *look, smell, feel, sound* und *taste* beschreiben in Sätzen mit Objekt eine Tätigkeit und können deshalb durch ein Adverb der Art und Weise näher bestimmt werden.
Beispiel:
She sounded the bell impatiently.
4. Die Übersetzung von *Wie sieht das aus?* ist entweder *How does it look?* oder *What does it look like?*
5. Das deutsche Wort *einzeln* kann im Englischen unterschiedlich wiedergegeben werden. Finden Sie die verschiedenen Übersetzungsäquivalente und bilden Sie je zwei Beispielsätze.
6. Nach *keep on* steht die Konstruktion Verb + *-ing* wie beispielsweise *keep on trying* oder *keep on dancing*.
7. *Umweltfreundlich* heißt im Englischen normalerweise entweder *environmentally friendly* oder *environment friendly*. Es finden sich aber auch Ausdrücke wie *ecologically friendly/beneficial*.
8. In der Regel heißt *hineintun, hineinsetzen, hineinlegen, hineinstellen* und *hineinstecken* im Englischen *put in* wie in *She put it in her bag* oder *He put it in his pocket*. Die Form mit *into* ist in diesem Zusammenhang sehr ungewöhnlich, sie würde die Richtung der Handlung in unverhältnismäßiger Weise verstärken. Die Form *put into* ist u.a. korrekt in Sätzen wie *Put it into Russian* oder *The ship put in(to) a harbour*.

Lernphase 2

1. Adjektive auf *-ic* und *-ical* bilden die Adverbform auf *-ally* wie beispielsweise *historic – historically* oder *economic/economical – economically*. Eine Ausnahme ist *publicly*.
2. Erklären Sie den Unterschied zwischen *We keep ourselves fit* bzw. *We keep fit* und *They keep us fit*.
3. *Sich von etwas ernähren* heißt im Englischen u.a. *feed on sth.* und *nourish oneself on sth.*

4. *Nicht mehr* kann im Englischen sowohl mit *no more* als auch mit *no longer* übersetzt werden. Geben Sie die Regeln an und finden Sie je zwei typische Beispiele.
5. Bei der Übersetzung von *allergisch gegen* werden oft zwei Fehler gemacht. Wie heißt die richtige Form im Englischen?
6. Sowohl *lung* als auch *lungs* ist im Englischen korrekt. Worin besteht der Unterschied?
7. Die richtige Übersetzung von *tragisch* lautet *tragic*.
8. Wie werden *fabric* und *motor* ins Deutsche übersetzt? Bilden Sie je zwei Beispielsätze. Wie wird das Wort *Stoff* (im Sinne von „Textil") ins Englische übersetzt? Bilden Sie zwei Beispielsätze.

Übungsphase 1

Übersetzen Sie ins Englische:
1. Sie sah glücklich aus.
2. Er sah seine Tochter glücklich an.
3. Dieses Gewebe besteht aus Nylon und Wolle.
4. Wir wissen jetzt, wie die Oberfläche des Mondes aussieht.
5. Die Umweltverschmutzung hat jetzt den Nordpol erreicht.
6. Sie ist ein Einzelkind.
7. Ein einzelner Baum stand in der Wüste.
8. Dieses Produkt ist umweltfreundlich.
9. Seine Lunge war gesund.

Übungsphase 2

Übersetzen Sie ins Englische:
1. Sie steckte das Buch in ihre Aktentasche.
2. Der Motor des Wagens war kaputt.
3. Sie trug Kleider, die auf beinahe komische Weise unpassend waren.
4. Unsere junge Tochter hält uns fit.
5. Er hält sich durch viel Joggen fit.
6. Viele Tiere ernähren sich von Pflanzen.
7. Ich trinke kein Bier mehr.
8. Ich bin gegen Pollen aller Art allergisch.
9. Sein Fall war tragisch.
10. Sie stellte dauernd Fragen.

Text 11

 Der folgende Text kann, muß aber nicht, typische Fehler deutschsprachiger Lernender enthalten. Lesen Sie den Text durch und markieren Sie die Stellen, die Ihrer Meinung nach falsch sind.

The Modern European

With the approach of 1992, when custom barriers will fall throughout Europe, great changes are to expect. One of these will concern people's attitudes towards language learning. In the moment, there is a proliferation of language learning in Europe. Ideally spoken, "the Eurocrat of 1992" will be like a Swiss – speaking at last three languages, ie his or her mother tongue, English and one other foreign language.
Bowing to feelings of national pride, the EC can boast no fewer than nine "official languages". But to limit its cost, the EC conducts most of its businesses in three "working languages": English, French and German. And in practice, English is the language of choice in commerce, science, technology, advertising and public relations.
However there are compelling reasons of executives and salespeople to be multilingual. For example, in a business deal, a German speaking English has a distinct advantage over an English person who does not speak German. Faced with an ever increasing economical concurrence within the EC, even the British are becoming convinced of the fact that foreign languages are vital for them. As a result, language schools are opening up overall in Britain, and in Europe as a whole, a well-known language school has doubled it's teaching load in the last five years.
The British have been notorious for their lack of interest in foreign languages, but now the advent of 1992 along with the construction of the Channel Tunnel seem to be eroding Britain's insularity. Britain can no longer afford to loose touch with this development and changes in the school curriculum will now make it compulsory for British schoolchildren to learn at last one foreign language up to the age of sixteen. With other words, the British are bowing to the inevitable.
A further question is how Europe's languages will fare after 1992. Some experts foresee the day when an Europeanised form of English – perhaps we could call it "Eurolish" – will be the common language in Europe. The smaller languages would fall into disuse. Other linguists see a danger of a regionalisation of languages and cultures, with some languages being restricted on rural areas. Yet others mean that by retaining nine official languages, the EC may have stopped the decline of smaller languages.

Haben Sie in dem Text Fehler gefunden? Zur Kontrolle bitte umblättern.

Fehlerkorrektur

Auf dieser Seite finden Sie die Liste der Fehler. Arbeiten Sie zunächst die Lern- und Übungsphasen durch und setzen Sie danach die korrekten Formen *im Sinnzusammenhang* in die dafür vorgesehenen Schreibräume unten ein.

1. * custom barriers: _____

2. * changes are to expect: _____

3. * in the moment: _____

4. * ideally spoken: _____

5. (*) at last three languages / (*) to learn at last one language: _____

6. (*) businesses: _____

7. * reasons of: _____

8. * economical: _____

9. (*) concurrence: _____

10. * vital for them: _____

11. * overall in Britain: _____

12. * it's teaching load: _____

13. * to loose touch: _____

14. * with other words: _____

15. * an Europeanised form: _____

16. * restricted on rural areas: _____

17. (*) others mean: _____

Lernphase 1

1. Schlagen Sie folgende Wörter in einem zweisprachigen Wörterbuch nach: *meinen* (im Sinne von „behaupten") und *Konkurrenz* sowie *mean* (v.) und *concurrence*. Bilden Sie jeweils einen Satz mit den englischen Wörtern.
2. *Zoll* heißt im Englischen *Customs/customs*. Dementspreched muß es *customs barriers, customs duty, customs buildings, customs house, customs clearance* und *Customs officer* heißen.
Merke: In einigen attributiv verwendeten Zusammensetzungen stehen auch Singularformen wie z.b. *a spectacle case, a trouser leg, a pyjama top* und *lung cancer*.
3. Vergleichen und erklären Sie die beiden Infinitivkonstruktionen: *Changes are difficult to bring about* und *Changes are to be brought about*.
4. *Im Moment* wird normalerweise mit *at the moment*, aber auch mit *at the present moment* oder *at this moment in time* übersetzt.
5. Wie bereits unter Text 1 besprochen, müssen **Partizipialkonstruktionen** als Entsprechung zu kommentierenden Adverbien im Englischen mit dem Partizip Präsens stehen, es muß also *ideally speaking* heißen.
6. *At last* und *at least* werden oft verwechselt. Übersetzen Sie die beiden Ausdrücke ins Deutsche.
Merke auch: *last but not least*.
7. Erklären Sie den Unterschied zwischen *a lot of business* und *a lot of businesses* und bilden Sie je zwei Sätze.
8. *Gründe für* heißt im Englischen *reasons for*.

Lernphase 2

1. Es besteht ein Bedeutungsunterschied zwischen *economic* und *economical*. Wie werden beide Wörter ins Deutsche übersetzt?
Merke: die Adverbform ist für beide Wörter gleich, nämlich *economically*.
2. Die korrekte Präposition nach *vital* ist *to*.
3. *Überall in Britannien* heißt entweder *everywhere in Britain, all over Britain* oder *in the whole of Britain*.
4. Meist als Flüchtigkeitsfehler erscheinen *it's* für *its* und *its* für *it's*. Bilden Sie jeweils zwei Sätze.
5. Merken Sie sich *lose* [luːz] (verlieren), *loosen* ['luːsn] (lösen, lockern) und *loose* [luːs] (lose, locker). Lesen oder transkribieren Sie die Sätze *The button is loose, I hate to lose buttons, Can you please loosen the buttons*.
6. *Mit anderen Worten* ist im Englischen *in other words*.
7. Unter Text 4 wurde bereits erklärt, daß es *a European* heißen muß. Korrekt ist deshalb *a Europeanized form*.
8. *Restricted to* ist die richtige Übersetzung von *begrenzt/beschränkt auf*.

Übungsphase 1

Übersetzen Sie ins Englische:
1. In den letzten Jahren sind in Europa einige Zollgrenzen gefallen.
2. In Osteuropa sind viele Veränderungen zu erwarten.
3. Idealerweise (gesagt) sollte jede(r) Europäer(in) mindestens zwei Sprachen sprechen.
4. Sie können mit uns Geschäfte machen.
5. Er leitet mehrere kleine Geschäfte (im Sinne von „Läden").
6. Der Grund für sein Verhalten war nicht klar.
7. Sie machten es aus wirtschaftlichen Gründen.
8. Diese Heizmethode ist sehr sparsam.
9. Es gibt sehr viel Konkurrenz aus dem Ausland.
10. Was für ein interessantes Zusammentreffen von Ereignissen.

Übungsphase 2

Übersetzen Sie ins Englische:
1. Es ist lebenswichtig für Tiere, daß sie ihrem Instinkt gehorchen.
2. Überall in Europa spricht man vom Ende des Kalten Krieges.
3. Es ist seine Idee.
4. Das ist der neueste Computer. Seine Leistung ist unschlagbar.
5. Er wollte seine Geduld nicht verlieren.
6. Zwei Knöpfe waren lose.
7. Mit anderen Worten, er war einfach zu faul, die Regeln zu lernen.
8. Endlich fanden wir heraus, was wirklich in jener Nacht geschehen war.
9. Es wird bald einen europäischen Paß geben.
10. Viele Leute behaupten, daß diese Krankheit auf eine Bevölkerungsschicht beschränkt ist.

Text 12

 Der folgende Text kann, muß aber nicht, typische Fehler deutschsprachiger Lernender enthalten. Lesen Sie den Text durch und markieren Sie die Stellen, die Ihrer Meinung nach falsch sind.

Crime Does Pay!

Even Hercule Poirot, that master of logic deduction, might be surprised at the continuing success of his creator, Agatha Christie. She remains the leader in tables of sales and royalties earned. Some persons claim that she has even outsold William Shakespeare himself. Agatha Christie's romans have become an English institution. She wrote eighty-four alltogether, in addition to nineteen pieces and four non-fictional books. 1990 is the centenary of her birth and will no doubt provide us with a whole year of commemoration and even larger sales.

Agatha Christie was quite a character herself, since her own life was something of a riddle. She is born in Devon. Her American father died as she was a child and her mother brought her up in true Edwardian style. It was the break-up of Agatha Christie's first wedding with Archibald Christie in 1928 which made her a household name. After learning of her man's involvement with another woman, she disappeared from home, causing a nationwide police search. She was found in a hotel in Harrogate registered under the name of her man's lover. The family claimed that she had suffered of amnesia, but the riddle has never been satisfactorily solved. Two years later, she married Max Mallowan, who was archaeologist. The pair traveled to Istanbul, Egypt and Baghdad, which provided the setting of many of her actions.

Agatha Christie died in 1976, leaving Agatha Christie Ltd. to her family, and her grandson now leads the firm.

An interesting question remains – how has Agatha Christie managed to retain her popularity for so long? Her literature agent claims that the presentation of her works on the film screen and in television has led to a revival. The film "Murder on the Orient Express" had already established the potential of the stories as vehicles for the nostalgia. He also believes that the style and the mundane atmosphere of the good old time in her books appealed to the public of the seventies and eighties. The West End piece "The Mousetrap" certainly testifies her continuing popularity – it is the longest-running piece in history, its debut having been in 1952.

Haben Sie in dem Text Fehler gefunden? Zur Kontrolle bitte umblättern.

Fehlerkorrektur

Auf dieser Seite finden Sie die Liste der Fehler. Arbeiten Sie zunächst die Lern- und Übungsphasen durch und setzen Sie danach die korrekten Formen *im Sinnzusammenhang* in die dafür vorgesehenen Schreibräume unten ein.

1. * logic deduction: _____
2. (*) some persons: _____
3. * romans: _____
4. * alltogether: _____
5. (*) nineteen pieces / * West End piece / * longest-running piece: _____

_____

_____

6. * she is born: _____
7. (*) as she was a child: _____
8. (*) first wedding: _____
9. * wedding with Archibald: _____
10. (*) her man's involvement / (*) her man's lover: _____

_____

11. * suffered of amnesia: _____
12. * who was archaeologist: _____
13. (*) the pair: _____
14. (*) traveled: _____
15. * the setting of: _____

16. * the setting of many of her actions: _____

17. (*) her grandson now leads the firm: _____

18. * her literature agent: _____
19. (*) her works: _____
20. * in television: _____
21. (*) the nostalgia: _____
22. (*) the mundane atmosphere: _____

23. * the good old time: _____
24. * testifies her popularity: _____

Lernphase 1

1. Schlagen Sie folgende Vokabeln in einem zweisprachigen Wörterbuch nach: *logisch, Roman, Stück* (im Sinne von „Theaterstück"), *ein Paar* (1. im Sinne von „Ehepaar", 2. im Sinne von „zwei") und *mondän*. Bilden Sie je einen Satz mit den englischen Entsprechungen.
2. Der Plural von *a person* ist normalerweise *people*. Wann wird *persons* verwendet?
3. Wie andere Zusammensetzungen mit *all-* wird auch *altogether* mit einem *l* geschrieben (vgl. *already, although, always*).
4. Bei der Frage *Wann sind Sie geboren?* und der Antwort *Ich bin 1971 geboren* steht im Englischen immer das **past**, da es sich um ein zu einem bestimmten Zeitpunkt in der Vergangenheit abgeschlossenes Geschehen handelt: *When were you born? I was born in 1971.*
5. Die temporale Konjunktion *als* heißt im Englischen *when*.
6. Wie werden *wedding* und *marriage* ins Deutsche übersetzt? Wie sagt man im Englischen *meine Heirat mit John?*

7. *Mein (Ehe-)Mann* heißt im Englischen normalerweise *husband* (infml.: *hubbie*). Manchmal wird auch *man* verwendet. Welches deutsche Wort entspricht hier dem englischen *man?*
8. Wie wird *leiden unter (einer Krankheit)* ins Englische übersetzt?
9. Bei dem Gebrauch des **unbestimmten Artikels** in Zusammenhang mit Berufsbezeichnungen werden oft Fehler gemacht. Wie wird *Ich bin Student* ins Englische übersetzt und wie lautet die Regel?
10. Im Englischen existiert sowohl die Form *traveled* als auch *travelled*. Welche Erklärung gibt es für beide Formen?

Lernphase 2

1. Merke: *logic* ist n i c h t *logisch,* englisch *roman/Roman* ist n i c h t deutsch *Roman* und *mundane* ist n i c h t *mondän.* Wie werden die vier englischen Wörter ins Deutsche übersetzt? Bilden Sie je einen englischen Satz mit diesen Wörtern.
2. Der *Schauplatz der Handlung/der Handlungen* ist im Englischen *the setting for the plot/plots.*
3. *Eine Firma leiten* heißt im Englischen *run a firm.* Andererseits ist ein Satz wie *He led the firm into bankruptcy* möglich.
4. Wie bereits unter Text 4 erläutert, ist die Konstruktion Nomen + Nomen im Englischen weniger häufig. Es muß also *literary agent* heißen.
5. Das Wort *Arbeit* bzw. *Arbeiten* bereitet Nichtmuttersprachlern in der englischen Sprache meist Schwierigkeiten. *Work* heißt im Deutschen *Arbeit* bzw. *Arbeiten.* *Homework* kann sowohl *Hausarbeit* als auch *Hausarbeiten* bedeuten. *Das ist eine gute Arbeit* wird dann mit *This is a good piece of work* übersetzt. *Works* wird im Englischen entweder im Sinne von *works of art* (Singular: *a work of art*) oder in Verbindungen wie *a gas works* und *a dye works* verwendet. Im obigen Kontext ist *work* wahrscheinlich angemessener, da nicht Agatha Christies Kunstwerke gemeint sind, sondern ihr Gesamtwerk.
6. *Im Fernsehen* ist im Englischen *on television* (infml.: *on telly*).
7. *Nostalgia* gehört im Englischen zu den Abstrakta und wird deshalb ohne Artikel gebraucht.
8. *The good old days* ist die korrekte Übersetzung von *die gute alte Zeit.*
9. *Eine Sache beweisen/bescheinigen* heißt im Englischen *testify to sth.* Andere Kollokationen sind *testify against sb./sth.* und *testify in favour of sb./sth.* Beispiele sind *The teacher testified to the girl's honesty, A married woman is not allowed to testify against her husband in court, She testified in favour of the accused.*
10. Nennen Sie vier verschiedene Bedeutungen von *as* als Konjunktion und bilden Sie je einen Beispielsatz.

Übungsphase 1

Übersetzen Sie ins Englische:
1. Es ist nur logisch, daß wir etwas gegen die Umweltverschmutzung tun müssen.
2. Alle anwesenden Personen wurden verhaftet.
3. Ich kann seiner Logik nicht folgen.
4. Sie schrieb zwölf Romane.
5. Die Römer besetzten ganz England.
6. Diese Spalte ist in Antiquaschrift gedruckt.
7. Insgesamt spielte er bei vierzehn Testspielen mit.
8. Sie hat ein neues Theaterstück geschrieben.
9. Als ich ein Kind war, waren die Dinge anders.

Übungsphase 2

Übersetzen Sie ins Englische:
1. Ich bin in London geboren.
2. Als ich jung war, reiste ich viel.
3. Es waren viele Gäste auf der Hochzeit.
4. Ihre Familie mißbilligte ihre Heirat mit John.
5. Der Ruf ihres Mannes war hervorragend.
6. Manchmal leide ich unter Kopfschmerzen.
7. Mein Freund ist Archäologe.
8. Sie sind ein nettes Paar.
9. Ich habe mir ein Paar neue Schuhe gekauft.
10. Der Schauplatz seiner Handlungen war immer Afrika.

Übungsphase 3

Übersetzen Sie ins Englische:
1. Sie führen ein kleines Hotel.
2. Wer ist ihr(e) Literaturagent(in)?
3. Shakespeares Werke werden nie an Popularität verlieren.
4. Ich habe meine Hausaufgaben beendet.
5. Wo ist das Gaswerk?
6. Haben Sie gestern die Premierministerin im Fernsehen gesehen?
7. Die Nostalgie vieler Leute für die sogenannte gute alte Zeit ist mir unverständlich.
8. Dieser Ort ist sehr mondän.
9. Er führte eine sehr schlichte und einfache Existenz.
10. Ihr nervöses Verhalten zeugte davon, daß sie schuldig war.
11. Die Nostalgie kann als bedeutendes Phänomen dieses Jahrzehnts angesehen werden.

Text 13

 Der folgende Text kann, muß aber nicht, typische Fehler deutschsprachiger Lernender enthalten. Lesen Sie den Text durch und markieren Sie die Stellen, die Ihrer Meinung nach falsch sind.

Young People in the Eighties

The results of a survey of young people's behaviour carried out in Britain have been summarised in an actual report entitled "Young People in 1987" and published by the Health Education Authority. It reveals that the differences between the sexes are greater than any changes in teenage behaviour over the past few years. A striking example for different masculine and feminine behaviour concerns drugs and pain killers. The survey shows that one of the most worrying features was that girls apparently employ far more pain killers than boys. Boys, however, are more involved in taking illegal drugs, although total numbers are very low. Less than one percent of young people between forteen and sixteen had taken heroin. Cannabis is still the most widely-used drug among teenagers.

As society expects that girls are slim, it is not surprising that girls are much more concerned about weight problems than boys. Till the time they are fifteen, two-thirds have made a diet at least once. Fewer boys try to slim and the trend decreases with age. Boys also consume more "junk food" as fizzy drinks and chocolate, while girls prefer fruit. Strangely enough, the most popular food or drink overall was fruit juice.

Further results show that the attitudes of boys and girls towards grooming and cleanliness are quiet different. Girls bath and brush the teeth more regularly than boys. Other distinctions can be seen in attitudes towards work and leisure activities. Boys spend much time seeing television, playing computer and slot machine games and "hanging about" in the street, whereas girls devote their time to do work for school or go to parties and discoes. Girls of all ages do more homeworks than boys. However, the number of teenagers who have stopped to do homeworks altogether increases between the ages of eleven and sixteen.

Girls, in contrast to boys, develop certain adult habits rather quickly, f.e. girls get used to drink alcohol and smoke rather early in life and are more likely to have a steady boy friend by the age of fifteen. Despite certain worrying factors, the report ends on an optimistic note by showing that smoking and drinking among teenagers has decreased overall and only a tiny fraction is involved in drug-taking. There is hope that this positive trend will continue in the next time.

Haben Sie in dem Text Fehler gefunden? Zur Kontrolle bitte umblättern.

Fehlerkorrektur

Auf dieser Seite finden Sie die Liste der Fehler. Arbeiten Sie zunächst die Lern- und Übungsphasen durch und setzen Sie danach die korrekten Formen *im Sinnzusammenhang* in die dafür vorgesehenen Schreibräume unten ein.

1. (*) actual report: _____

2. * example for: _____

3. (*) masculine and feminine behaviour: _____
   _____

4. * girls employ pain killers: _____
   _____

5. * forteen: _____

6. * society expects that girls are slim: _____
   _____

7. * till the time they are fifteen: _____
   _____

8. * two-thirds have made a diet: _____
   _____

9. * "junk food" as fizzy drinks: _____
   _____

10. * quiet different: _____

11. * girls brush the teeth: _____

12. * boys spend much time: _____

13. * seeing television: _____

14. * girls devote their time to do work for school or go: _____

---

15. * discoes: _____

16. * girls do more homeworks / * to do homeworks: _____

---

17. (*) who have stopped to do: _____

---

18. * f.e.: _____

19. * girls get used to drink alcohol and smoke: _____

---

20. * boy friend: _____

21. * in the next time: _____

Lernphase 1

1. Schlagen Sie das Wort *aktuell* in einem zweisprachigen Wörterbuch nach und bilden Sie mit Hilfe eines einsprachigen Wörterbuches für jedes englische Wort je einen Beispielsatz.
2. Was heißt *actual(ly)* auf deutsch?
3. *Beispiel für* heißt im Englischen *example of.*
4. Wie unterscheiden sich *male, masculine* und *manly* im Englischen? Bilden Sie jeweils einen Satz.
5. Wann gebraucht man im Englischen *female, feminine, womanly* und *effiminate?* Bilden Sie jeweils einen Satz.
6. *Medikamente (ein)nehmen* wird im Englischen mit *take medicaments/ medicine/drugs* oder *use medicaments/drugs* übersetzt. Es heißt also *take pain killers* oder *use pain killers.*

7. Korrigieren Sie die Schreibungen *forteen, (*)quiet („ziemlich, ganz") und *boy friend.
8. Welche Konstruktion steht im Englischen nach erwarten, daß ...? Übersetzen Sie den Satz Ich erwarte, daß sie ihre Pflicht tut ins Englische.

Lernphase 2
1. Merke: actual ist n i c h t aktuell.
2. Bis kann im Englischen mit till/until und by übersetzt werden. Erklären Sie den unterschiedlichen Gebrauch und bilden Sie je einen Satz.
3. Eine Diät machen heißt im Englischen diet, be on a diet oder go on a diet.
4. Finden Sie zwei Übersetzungsäquivalente für wie (im Sinne von „zum Beispiel") im Englischen. Bilden Sie je zwei Beispielsätze.
5. Quiet und quite sind im Englischen phonetisch sehr ähnlich, deshalb kommt es oft zu falschen Schreibungen. Merke: She is quite good at French. He is quiet.
6. Es muß They brush their teeth heißen, da anders als im Deutschen das attributive Possessivpronomen im Englischen auch verwendet wird, um ein Zugehörigkeitsverhältnis bei Körperteilen (und Kleidungsstücken sowie bei Wörtern wie life und mind) zu bezeichnen. Andere Beispiele sind She shook her head und He put his hands in his pockets.
7. Viel heißt im Englischen a lot of und much. Der Gebrauch der beiden Wörter ist wie folgt: 1. In positiven Aussagesätzen steht in der Regel a lot of, lots of (infml.) oder plenty of; 2. In Fragen und negativen Aussagesätzen steht in der Regel much.
Beispiele:
The singer earned a lot of money.
She likes plenty of butter.
There is not much milk left in the jug.
Is there much money in this business?

Lernphase 3
1. Watch television/TV/telly (infml.) ist die korrekte Übersetzung von fernsehen.
2. Welche verbale Konstruktion erfolgt nach devote to?
3. Bilden Sie den Plural von grotto, ghetto, studio, radio, echo, potato, veto, cargo und volcano. Welche Regeln lassen sich für diese Fälle aufstellen?
4. Wie wird Hausarbeiten ins Englische übersetzt (s. Text 12, Lernphase 2, Nummer 5)?
5. I stopped to drink wine und I stopped drinking wine sind beide korrekt, haben aber eine verschiedene Bedeutung. Übersetzen Sie die beiden Sätze ins Deutsche.
6. Die Abkürzung e.g. bzw. eg steht für for example.
7. Welche verbale Konstruktion erfolgt nach get used to (s. Text 8, Lernphase 1, Nummer 5)? Bilden Sie zwei Beispielsätze.
8. Wie übersetzen Sie in nächster Zeit ins Englische?

Übungsphase 1

Übersetzen Sie ins Englische:
1. Die eigentlichen Kosten waren viel höher als wir erwartet hatten.
2. Sie interessiert sich für die aktuellen Ereignisse in Osteuropa.
3. Diese Kirche ist ein klassisches Beispiel für die mittelalterliche Architektur.
4. Viele Frauen wollen einige typisch männliche Haltungen ändern.
5. Er hat eine eher weibliche Stimme.
6. Er sieht sehr männlich in seiner neuen Uniform aus.
7. Der Arzt sagte mir, ich solle drei Tabletten vor jeder Mahlzeit nehmen.
8. Er war erst vierzehn.

Übungsphase 2

Übersetzen Sie ins Englische:
1. Wir erwarten, daß er um 11 Uhr zurück ist.
2. Bis morgen werden sie eine Entscheidung getroffen haben.
3. Warte, bis ich komme.
4. Im Januar mache ich immer eine Diät.
5. Als Franzose ist er gutes Essen gewohnt.
6. Südeuropäer wie z.B. Italiener und Spanier gebrauchen ihre Hände mehr beim Sprechen.
7. In diesem Jahr ist alles ganz anders.
8. Ich putze mir die Zähne regelmäßig.

Übungsphase 3

Übersetzen Sie ins Englische:
1. Ich habe viel Arbeit zu tun.
2. Ich sehe gern fern, wenn ich müde bin.
3. Studenten sollten dem Lesen mehr Zeit widmen.
4. Im letzten Jahr hat sie aufgehört, in Discos zu gehen.
5. Kein Schüler mag Hausaufgaben.
6. Meine Freundin gewöhnt sich langsam daran, weniger zu arbeiten.
7. Viele von meinen Freundinnen werden studieren, z.B. Janine, Sabine, Doris und Natascha.
8. In der nächsten Zeit wird mein Freund heiraten.

Text 14

 Der folgende Text kann, muß aber nicht, typische Fehler deutschsprachiger Lernender enthalten. Lesen Sie den Text durch und markieren Sie die Stellen, die Ihrer Meinung nach falsch sind.

School in West Germany

A group of professors from the Lüneburg University in the Federal Republic of Germany recently revealed some of the results of a survey carried out among German school children. The children were asked to give their opinions about teachers, syllabuses and notes in the form of written essays. Seven thousand in Lower Saxony and Bavaria were involved in the survey as well as a comparative group of five thousand pupils from Sweden, England and the United States.

The results of this survey indicate that notes, school reports and competitive pression to succeed weight heavily on German pupils – the more so the older they are. Some of the phrases used by pupils in their essays to describe school were "a prison", "a cage", "an institution which swallows up imaginary children and turns them out at the other end all in the same uniform grey which characterises the school building".

The main critic of the syllabus was that it was too theoretical. And a large number of pupils see tests and the resultant notes as their "greatest ennemy". In the eleventh class, 55.5% of the pupils suffer under stress associated with pression to succeed. 42.6% of all grammar school pupils criticise the system of notes. Notes seem to be especially injust for pupils, since class tests are usually not evaluated objectively. In addition, oral work, which plays a dominant role in determining the end note, is also assessed subjectively by the teacher. On the one side, this system encourages pupils to do everything to "get in with" the teacher, on the other side it creates frust, mistrust and even disgust in quite a number of young people, who feel that they are treated unfair. Comparative numbers from abroad show that notes at least must not be such a source of dissatisfaction. In West Germany, 27.8% of the pupils esteem notes negatively, whereas in Sweden this number is 10.6%, in the United States 4.3% and in England only 2.1%.

The motivation experienced by German pupils is correspondingly low. Only 12.7% of secondary school pupils and 18.8% of those at grammar schools actually like going to school. It is certainly symptomatic that sport, art and music are the pupils' favorite topics with physic and chemistry at the bottom of the list.

Haben Sie in dem Text Fehler gefunden? Zur Kontrolle bitte umblättern.

Fehlerkorrektur

Auf dieser Seite finden Sie die Liste der Fehler. Arbeiten Sie zunächst die Lern- und Übungsphasen durch und setzen Sie danach die korrekten Formen *im Sinnzusammenhang* in die dafür vorgesehenen Schreibräume unten ein.

1. * the Lüneburg University: _____
2. * school children: _____
3. (*) notes: _____
4. * pression: _____
5. (*) weight heavily: _____
6. (*) imaginary children: _____
7. (*) critic: _____
8. * ennemy: _____
9. * suffer under stress: _____
10. * injust: _____
11. * injust for: _____
12. * end note: _____
13. * on the one side / (*) on the other side: _____
_____
14. * frust: _____
15. * treated unfair: _____
16. (*) comparative numbers: _____
17. (*) must not: _____

18. * esteem negatively: _____

19. (*) favorite: _____

20. (*) topics: _____

21. (*) physic: _____

Lernphase 1

1. Schlagen Sie in einem zweisprachigen Wörterbuch folgende Wörter nach: *Noten* (1. „Schulnoten", 2. „Musiknoten"), *Kritik* und *Physik*. Bilden Sie mit jedem Wort je einen englischen Satz.
2. *Die Universität von Newcastle* heißt im Englischen *Newcastle University* bzw. *The University of Newcastle*.
3. Wie werden im Englischen *Schulkinder, Lieblingsfach* und *Feind* geschrieben?
4. *Druck* heißt hier *pressure*.
5. Welcher Unterschied besteht zwischen *weight* (v.) und *weigh*?
6. Finden Sie die Bedeutungen von *imaginable, imaginary* und *imaginative*.
7. Im Englischen heißt es *suffer from an illness/shock/stress*.
8. Im Englischen finden Sie *injustice* als Nomen und *unjust* als Adjektiv. Man sagt *do sb. an injustice* und *be unjust to sb.*
9. Die *Endnote* bzw. *Endzensur* wird im Englischen durch die Verbindung Adjektiv + Nomen wiedergegeben. Die korrekte Übersetzung lautet *final mark*.

Lernphase 2

1. Merke: *notes* ist n i c h t *(Schul)Noten* und *critic* ist n i c h t *Kritik*. Was bedeuten *notes* und *critic?*
2. Was heißt *auf der einen Seite* („einerseits") und *auf der anderen Seite* („andererseits") im Englischen? Wie übersetzen Sie *on one side* und *on the other side* ins Deutsche?
3. Eine Kurzform für *Frustration* gibt es nicht im Englischen. Die Übersetzung von *Frust* ist *frustration*.
4. Es existiert im Standardenglischen die unveränderliche Adjektivform *fair* in der Kollokation *play fair*, ansonsten muß aber die Adverbform genommen werden wie in *treat somebody fairly/unfairly*.
5. *Vergleichszahlen* heißt im Englischen *comparative figures*.
6. Wie übersetzen Sie ins Englische *nicht müssen, nicht brauchen* und *nicht dürfen?*
7. *Einschätzen/schätzen* kann im Englischen u.a. mit *esteem, respect, appreciate* und *regard* übersetzt werden. Erklären Sie die Unterschiede und bilden Sie je einen englischen Beispielsatz.

8. Wie unterscheiden sich *topic* und *subject?*
9. Wie übersetzen Sie *physics* und *physique* ins Deutsche?

Übungsphase 1
Übersetzen Sie ins Englische:
1. Ich studiere an der Universität von Keele.
2. Die Aula füllte sich schnell mit Schulkindern.
3. Fast alle Schulkinder erreichten eine sehr gute Note.
4. Ich kann die hohen Noten nicht singen.
5. Der Druck war unerträglich.
6. Sein letztes Argument wog schwer.
7. Sie ist eine sehr phantasievolle Studentin.
8. Viele Kinder entwickeln Ängste vor imaginären Gefahren.
9. Wir versuchten jedes denkbare Mittel, aber wir versagten am Ende.

Übungsphase 2
Übersetzen Sie ins Englische:
1. Was haben die Londoner Kritiker über den neuen Film gesagt?
2. Sie ist einer der gefürchtetsten Feinde des Regimes.
3. Jeder scheint unter zuviel Streß zu leiden.
4. Die Entscheidungen der Regierung sind für viele Frauen ungerecht.
5. Die Endzensur ist immer entscheidend.
6. Einerseits wird mein Job gut bezahlt, anderseits muß ich viele Stunden arbeiten.
7. Das Leben ist manchmal voller Frust.
8. Ich frage mich, warum sie ihn unfair behandelt.
9. Haben Sie irgendwelche Vergleichszahlen?

Übungsphase 3
Übersetzen Sie ins Englische:
1. Wir müssen nicht zu diesem Treffen gehen.
2. Sie dürfen diese Linie nicht übertreten.
3. Ich habe ihn immer hoch eingeschätzt.
4. Wer ist dein Lieblingsschauspieler?
5. Ich habe drei Fächer für meine mündliche Prüfung gewählt.
6. Politik oder Religion sind immer interessante Gesprächsthemen.
7. Ich hasse Physik.
8. Sein Körperbau ist großartig.

Text 15

 Der folgende Text kann, muß aber nicht, typische Fehler deutschsprachiger Lernender enthalten. Lesen Sie den Text durch und markieren Sie die Stellen, die Ihrer Meinung nach falsch sind.

Communicating I

The English word "communicate" means "to give" or "to share" – usually information and ideas. We may communicate to cooperate with others, to attract them, persuade them, organise them or control them. Our main means of communicating is of course the spoken and written word, and most people would accept that it is primarily the word's function to communicate ideas. But a surprising fact is that some experts believe that we communicate as many as 65% of our ideas and feelings without words and that we are very influenced by people's nonverbal behaviour. What is meant by this? Well, our physical appearance, the movements and gestures we make, how near we stand to each other or whether we touch each other – all these are part of communicating.

Some nonverbal behaviour, eg smiling, laughing, crying and showing fear, is similar all over the world, but some is not. Most people would probably agree that the English do not use so many gestures and speak slower than Southern Europeans. On the other hand, some gestures are used in common by various nations, but with different meanings. If a person taps the side of his or her head, he or she may mean that you are intelligent – or plain silly! If people shake their head horizontally from side to side, this usually means "no". However, in Greece, a very similar gesture means "yes" and can easily lead to misunderstandings.

A British anthropologist, Desmond Morris, examined the use of twenty different gestures in forty places in Europe. One of these was the "head toss". The head is tossed quickly upward and backward, often with the eyes closed, then lowered more slowly. His data shows that people in some parts of Europe do not use this gesture at all; some people in other parts use it to mean "yes"; and in still other areas the gesture has other meanings. British, German or Scandinavian holidaymakers in Italy are sometimes very disturbed and even offended by this gesture, imagining the other person to mean that he or she is superior. Being a time of extensive travel, people all over the world must try and keep an open mind regarding these matters. They must learn that communicative behaviour is culture-bound.

Haben Sie in dem Text Fehler gefunden? Zur Kontrolle bitte umblättern.

Fehlerkorrektur

Der Text enthält k e i n e Fehler. Lesen Sie sich die Anmerkungen zu den einzelnen *items* durch.

1. cooperate
2. organise
3. the word's function
4. very influenced
5. nonverbal
6. eg
7. speak slower
8. person ... his or her head/he or she
9. plain silly
10. people shake their head
11. tossed upward and backward
12. his data shows
13. very disturbed
14. being a time of extensive travel, people all over the world
15. people must try and keep
16. people must try and keep an open mind

Lernphase 1

1. Beide Schreibweisen, *co-operate* und *cooperate,* sind korrekt.
2. Ebenfalls sind die beiden Schreibungen *organize* und *organise* im BE üblich und korrekt.
3. Neben *the function of a word* ist *the word's function* möglich und korrekt: "The genitive is further used with certain kinds of inanimate nouns ... NOUNS 'OF SPECIAL RELEVANCE TO HUMAN ACTIVITY', eg: ... in *freedom's* name, *the book's* true importance ... *a word's* function, *the poll's* results, *television's* future ..." (CGEL, 324).
4. Die Korrektheit von *very influenced* hängt davon ab, ob *influenced* schon adjektivischen Status erlangt hat, da *influenced* als Partizip mit *(very) much* modifiziert wird. Mit der folgenden Einschränkung kann in diesem Fall ein adjektivischer Charakter angenommen werden: "... with the -ed participle, there appears to be divided usage, with increasing acceptance of the cooccurrence of *very* with a *by*-agent phrase containing a personal agent ..." (CGEL, 415).
5. Neben der Schreibung *non-verbal* tritt die andere korrekte Form *nonverbal* in verstärktem Maße auf.
6. Bei Abkürzungen wie beispielsweise *M.A., Ph.D., Dr., i.e.* und *e.g.* wurde früher in der Regel ein Punkt hinter die Buchstaben gesetzt. Diese Regelung erscheint heutzutage redundant, deshalb wird auf den Punkt im BE meistens verzichtet und einfach *MA, PhD, Dr, ie* und *eg* geschrieben.

7. Neben *speak more slowly* ist auch *speak slower* korrekt: "... the comparative and superlative forms of some adjectives are common also in standard English. ... Speak *clearer*. ['more clearly'] ... The car went *slower and slower*" (CGEL, 406).
8. Wie bereits erwähnt, finden sich in vielen (formellen) Texten die korrekten Formen *his and/or her* oder *he and/or she,* um einer eventuellen sexistischen Diskriminierung zu begegnen oder um bewußt auf Frauenbelange aufmerksam zu machen.

Lernphase 2

1. Der Ausdruck *plain silly* gehört natürlich dem informellen Stil an, er kann aber in dem Textzusammenhang "... you are intelligent – or plain silly!" durchaus benutzt und noch als korrekt eingestuft werden (s. CGEL, 446).
2. Zu erwarten wäre die Form *people shake their heads.* Abweichend von dieser Norm ist es aber auch möglich, den Singular zu gebrauchen, wenn der Schwerpunkt auf dem Einzelfall liegen soll: "While the distributive plural is the norm, the distributive singular may also be used to focus on individual instances. We therefore often have a number choice:
The students raised their *hand(s)*. ...
The exercise was not good for their *back(s)*" (CGEL, 768).
3. Präskriptivisten weisen auf die lateinische Pluralform von *data* hin und fordern deshalb auch eine entsprechende pluralische Verbform. Allerdings setzt sich die Interpretation des Wortes *data* als Singular immer mehr durch, so daß *data is* heutzutage ebenfalls als korrekt angesehen wird: "data ... is often constructed also as a singular, especially in scientific contexts ... *Much* of *this data* is inconclusive" (CGEL, 310).
4. Das Ableitungssuffix *-wards* oder *-ward* existiert in diesen beiden Formen. Die letztere Form findet sich besonders im (gedruckten) AE und gewinnt im BE immer mehr an Einfluß (s. CGEL, 438). Beide Formen sind korrekt, ein Mischen von AE und BE, sofern es überhaupt eindeutig feststellbar ist, könnte unter Umständen als stilistische Ungeschicklichkeit gewertet werden.
5. Der Fall *very disturbed* ist mit dem Fall *very influenced* zu vergleichen. Zusätzlich findet sich in modernen englischen Wörterbüchern für das Wort *disturbed* schon die Kennzeichnung als *adj.* (Adjektiv).
6. Das Beispiel *being a time of extensive travel, people all over the world* kann als „unverbundene Partizipialkonstruktion" ("unrelated, unattached or dangling participle") interpretiert werden. Was die Korrektheit dieser Konstruktionen betrifft, so ist zu bemerken, daß diese Grenzfälle darstellen. Vor allem dort, wo das implizierte Subjekt deutlich erkennbar ist, sollte heutzutage von korrekten Sätzen gesprochen werden. Außerdem sind bereits vier Fälle aufgeführt, bei denen die Korrektheit von Sätzen kaum noch in Frage gestellt wird:

"The attachment rule does not apply, or at least is relaxed, in certain cases:
a) The clause is a style disjunct ..., in which case the implied subject is the subject of the implied clause of speaking, normally I: *Putting it mildly,* you have caused us some inconvenience ...
b) The implied subject is the whole of the matrix clause: I'll help you *if necessary* ...
c) If the implied subject is an indefinite pronoun or prop *it* ..., the construction is considered less objectionable: *... Being Christmas,* the government offices were closed. ...
d) In formal scientific writing, the construction has become institutionalized where the implied subject is to be identified with the *I, we,* and *you* of the writer(s) or reader(s): *... To check on the reliability of the first experiment,* the experiment was replicated with a second set of subjects" (CGEL, 1122-1123). Der Satz in Text 15 entspricht der unter (c) aufgeführten Regel und ist dementsprechend als korrekt einzustufen.
7. Mit kleinen Bedeutungsunterschieden folgt dem Verb *try* der Infinitiv mit *to* oder das Gerundium (*-ing*), z.B. *try to do* und try *doing*. Da die Konstruktion *try to do* auch koordinierende Funktion haben kann, ist im informellen Englisch auch die Konstruktion *try and do* zu finden (s. CGEL, 507, 978-979). Die Form *try and keep* ist somit korrekt.
8. Im Falle des Ausdrucks *keep an open mind* ist der Plural *minds* ungewöhnlich, da es sich hier um einen mehr oder weniger festen Ausdruck handelt: "The singular is sometimes obligatory or preferable with idioms and metaphors:
We are *keeping an open mind.* [?*open minds*] ...
They can't *put their finger on* what's wrong. [*their fingers]" (CGEL, 768).

Text 15 kann aufgrund der obigen Ausführungen als völlig korrekt *(acceptable)* angesehen werden. Nur wenn ein formelles, geschriebenes Englisch gefordert ist, sind einige *items* stilistisch unangebracht *(inappropriate)*, nicht aber inkorrekt *(unacceptable)*.

Übersetzen Sie die folgenden Sätze ins Englische. Verwenden Sie formelle und informelle Formen, gebräuchliche und weniger gebräuchliche Formen, Varianten sowie BE und AE, soweit dies möglich ist.

Übungsphase 1

1. Verschiedene Länder arbeiteten zusammen, um ein neues Flugzeug zu bauen.
2. Er muß sein Leben ein bißchen besser organisieren.
3. Die Funktion dieses Wortes ist ziemlich eingeschränkt.
4. Junge Leute werden manchmal von Popsängern sehr beeinflußt.
5. Die nonverbale Kommunikation ist oft sehr schwer zu interpretieren.

6. Du mußt süße Speisen wie z.B. Kuchen, Eis und Pudding vermeiden.
7. Bei Schnee und Eis fahre ich langsamer.
8. C. Ferguson? Ich kenne diese Person nicht. Können Sie mir sagen, wo sie wohnt?

Übungsphase 2
1. Ihre Bemerkung war einfach dumm.
2. Sie schüttelten den Kopf, als sie die Nachricht hörten.
3. Die Daten werden im Büro für die Volkszählung noch geprüft.
4. Er sah zum Himmel auf.
5. Er muß sehr verstört gewesen sein.
6. Wenn man im Restaurant speist, sind Anzug und Krawatte vorgeschrieben.
7. Versuche, ruhig zu bleiben.
8. Die Mitglieder des Komitees versuchen, immer unvoreingenommen zu sein, und sind bereit, neue Ideen in Betracht zu ziehen.

Text 16

 Der folgende Text kann, muß aber nicht, typische Fehler deutschsprachiger Lernender enthalten. Lesen Sie den Text durch und markieren Sie die Stellen, die Ihrer Meinung nach falsch sind.

Communicating II

Another important source of information about a person is his or her face and especially the eyes. If you look at another person's eyes a lot while a conversation, people will think that you are open, friendly and self-conscious. If you avoid to look at the other person, you will be considered as cold and defensive. Southern Europeans look at each other more than Northern Europeans. Thus Italians might find English people serious and cold, whereas English people may find Italians sympathetic – neither of which may be the case.

In an ordinary conversation, we spend about a third of the time looking at each other, and this eye contact follows a certain pattern. If we deviate of this pattern, it will communicate a special meaning. For example, if we are nervous of someone, we do not look at them much. We stare at someone when we are angry or anxious, and longer eye contact than normal suggests that we are attracted to the other person.

Another aspect of communication concerns the question of room. People usually like to mark their personal room. For example, on the beach you may spread out a towel, or in a train you often put a bag or a coat on the seat next to you.

An interresting aspect of this is the physical distance people put between one another when talking. An American psychologist has found that when conversing, American males stand approximately fifty centimetres distant from another man, and sixty centimetres distant from a woman. If they are closer than this, they are either very agressive or very friendly. However, in South America or the Middle East, people stand much closer than this when conversing and are much more likely to touch themselves than the British for exemple.

These few examples show that language behaviour cannot be studied independant on people's socio-cultural backgrounds. Consequently, language learners should check these socio-cultural conventions. Knowing that these conventions exist can help to avoid misunderstandings in communication.

Haben Sie in dem Text Fehler gefunden? Zur Kontrolle bitte umblättern.

Fehlerkorrektur

Auf dieser Seite finden Sie die Liste der Fehler. Arbeiten Sie zunächst die Lern- und Übungsphasen durch und setzen Sie danach die korrekten Formen *im Sinnzusammenhang* in die dafür vorgesehenen Schreibräume unten ein.

1. (*) while a conversation: _____
2. (*) self-conscious: _____
3. * you avoid to look: _____
4. * considered as cold: _____
5. (*) sympathetic: _____
6. * we deviate of: _____
7. * for exemple / * exemples: _____
8. (*) the question of room / * their personal room: _____
   _____
9. * interresting: _____
10. * fifty/sixty centimetres distant from: _____
    _____
11. * agressive: _____
12. (*) to touch themselves: _____
13. * independant: _____
14. * independant on: _____
15. * cannot be studied independant: _____
    _____
16. (*) learners should check: _____

Lernphase 1

1. Schlagen Sie folgende Vokabeln in einem zweisprachigen Wörterbuch nach: *selbstbewußt* und *sympathisch*.
2. Wie übersetzen Sie *self-conscious* und *sympathetic* ins Deutsche?
3. Je nach Wortart wird *während* im Englischen mit *during* (Präpostion) oder *while* (Konjunktion) übersetzt. Es heißt also *while a conversation was going on* ... und *people look at each other during a conversation*. Bilden Sie je zwei Beispielsätze.
4. Das Verb *avoid* erlaubt folgende Konstruktionen: *avoid sth./sb.* und *avoid doing sth.*
5. *Jn. als dumm ansehen/betrachten* kann im Englischen u.a. mit *consider sb. (to be) foolish, regard sb. as foolish, think sb. foolish* (very fml.) und *count sb. (as) foolish* übersetzt werden.
6. *Abweichen von etwas* ist im Englischen *deviate from sth*.
7. Wie werden im Englischen *Beispiel, interessant, aggressiv* und *unabhängig* geschrieben?

Lernphase 2

1. *Self-conscious* ist n i c h t *selbstbewußt* und *sympathetic* ist n i c h t *sympathisch*.
2. *Raum* kann im Englischen u.a. mit *room* und *space* wiedergegeben werden. Wie werden die beiden englischen Wörter verwendet (s. Text 5, Lernphase 1, Nummer 5)? Bilden Sie je einen Beispielsatz.
3. *Zwei Kilometer entfernt von* heißt im Englischen u.a. *two kilometres (away) from*.
4. Erklären Sie den Unterschied zwischen *they touched themselves* und *they touched each other*.
5. *Unabhängig* ist im obigen Satz ein Adverb, es muß also *cannot be studied independently* heißen.
6. Merke: *be dependent on* und *be independent of*.
7. Das neudeutsche Wort *(ab)schecken* hat nicht dieselbe Bedeutung wie das englische Verb *check*. Bilden Sie jeweils zwei englische Sätze mit *understand* („begreifen") und *check* („überprüfen").

Übungsphase 1

Übersetzen Sie ins Englische:
1. Während der Operation fiel ein Student in Ohnmacht.
2. Während die Verhandlungen noch andauerten, begann das Schießen wieder.
3. Viele Schauspieler sind schüchtern, aber selbstbewußt.
4. In dieser Situation fühlte er sich befangen.
5. Sie vermied es, ihn anzusehen.
6. Er wurde als rachsüchtig angesehen.

7. Sie ist sehr sympathisch.
8. Er ist mir sympathisch.
9. Sie zeigte großes Mitgefühl, als sie von dem Unfall hörte.

Übungsphase 2

Übersetzen Sie ins Englische:
1. Er weicht nie von seinen Gewohnheiten ab. Zum Beispiel raucht er immer nach dem Mittagessen.
2. Wir haben nicht genug Raum/Platz für alle neuen Bücher.
3. Am Strand traf ich einige interessante Leute.
4. Er stand zehn Meter entfernt von mir.
5. Er ist eine sehr aggressive Person.
6. Faß mich nicht an!
7. Sie müssen lernen, unabhängig zu handeln.
8. Indien wurde 1947 von Großbritannien unabhängig.
9. Ich begreife/schecke einfach nicht, warum sie den Reifendruck nicht überprüft hat.

LÖSUNGSTEIL

Text 1

Fehlerkorrektur

1. *always*   2. *students' performance*   3. *a/one hundred*   4. *per cent/percent*
5. *have difficulty (in) recognizing*   6. *overlook*   7. *cannot blame the students either*
8. *typical of*   9. *make mistakes*   10. *frankly speaking*   11. *it is high time*   12. *correct texts properly*   13. *developed*   14. *a heavy smoker*   15. *Athens*   16. *carry coals to Newcastle*

Lernphase 1

1. typisch für = *typical of;* Fehler machen = *make mistakes;* es ist höchste Zeit = *it is high time* (Verb steht danach im past!); Eulen nach Athen tragen = *carry coals to Newcastle;* übersehen = *overlook, miss*
2. – –
3. Im Singular steht nach dem Nomen ein Apostroph, danach folgt ein *s*. Bei Wörtern, die den Plural auf *-s* bilden, folgt der Apostroph dem *s*.
   Beispiele: *the boy's coat, the girls' hats.*
   Bei Wörtern, die den Plural auf *-n* bilden, wird nach dem Wort ein Apostroph gesetzt, danach das *s*.
   Beispiele: *men's trousers; children's toys.*
   Bei Eigennamen auf *-s* steht vorzugsweise ein Apostroph und ein *s*, häufig aber nur ein Apostroph.
   Beispiele: *Dickens's/Dickens' novels; Mr Jones's/Mr Jones' house.*
4. Anders als im Deutschen kann im Englischen der unbestimmte Artikel bei 100 und 1000 nicht weggelassen werden. Im Singular heißt es im Englischen immer *a hundred* und *a thousand* bzw. betont *one hundred* und *one thousand.*
5. „Prozent" ist im Englischen *per cent* oder *percent.*
6. – –

Lernphase 2

1. a) *I can't swim either.*
   b) *Neither can my friend* bzw. *Nor can my friend* oder *My friend can't either.*
2. – –
3. Richtig kann u.a. mit *right* (oft: „was recht oder angebracht ist"), *correct* (oft: „fehlerfrei in Übereinstimmung mit einem Standard oder der Wahrheit") und *proper* (oft: „passend, wie es sich gehört, recht") übersetzt werden.
   right: right thing/train/people/man/woman/place
   correct: correct pronunciation/grammar/manners/dress/behaviour
   proper: proper study of mankind/word/course/doctor/job

4. Endkonsonaten werden in der Regel bei zwei- und mehrsilbigen Wörtern vor vokalisch anlautender Silbe verdoppelt, wenn die letzte Silbe des Basiswortes betont ist.
   Beispiele: *pre'fer – preferred, re'gret – regretting, under'cut – undercutting*
   Das Wort *de'velop* wird nicht auf der letzten Silbe betont, deshalb muß es *developing* und *developed* heißen.
   Neben einigen Ausnahmen sind vor allem Wörter auf *-l* zu nennen, die im BE (nicht aber im AE) den Endkonsonanten verdoppeln wie beispielsweise *travelled* oder *travelling*.
5. Einige Beispiele für Kollokationen sind:
   Adjektiv + Nomen
   beautiful girl/woman/lake/sunset – handsome man/woman (= good-looking in a strong, healthy way)/reward/gesture
   Verb + Nomen
   do a lot of damage/one's duty/wrong – make trouble/a lot of noise/one's bed
   Präposition + Nomen
   in the street/field/picture/country
6. – –
7. Athen = *Athens;* Brüssel = *Brussels;* Marseille = *Marseille/Marseilles;* Neapel = *Naples*

Übungsphase 1

1. *She has always loved him.*
2. *The pupils'/students' pronunciation is quite bad.*
3. *It is typical of him to be impolite.*
4. *You have made several spelling mistakes.*
5. *I cannot (come) either./Neither can I./Nor can I.*
6. *Non-natives often have difficulty (in) pronouncing English correctly.*
7. *Legally speaking, the government has/have not made a mistake.*
8. *Frankly speaking, he is simply not honest.*

Übungsphase 2

1. *It is high time (that) we sold the car.*
2. *She did not pronounce the sentence correctly.*
3. *If you want to learn English properly, you should go to England.*
4. *As Geoffrey rightly said, the arts are often underfinanced.*
5. *The film was developed in one day.*
6. *He is a heavy smoker.*
7. *carry coals to Newcastle*
8. *I am competent enough to use English proverbs properly/correctly.*
9. *Poland is 90 per cent/percent Catholic.*

Text 2

Fehlerkorrektur

1. *I read ... recently* 2. *phenomenon* 3. *grammar school* 4. *received/got*
5. *grant/scholarship* 6. *information* 7. *good at geography* 8. *has affected*
9. *his studies* 10. *most of his essays* 11. *all (that)* 12. *taking his exams*

Lernphase 1

1. Phänomen = *phenomenon*, (pl.) *phenomena*, Gymnasium = *grammar school* (BE), *high school* (AE), Stipendium = *grant, scholarship* (im Sinne von „Preis").
2. *I paid my debts recently. I recently published a new book.* („vor kurzem", englisch auch *not long ago*) – *What have you been doing recently? I have not seen her recently.* („in letzter Zeit")
3. Typische Konstruktionen mit werden sind im Englischen:
   become angry/famous/a habit/a teacher;
   come apart/true/open/loose;
   fall ill/asleep/a victim to;
   get cold/drunk/tired/old;
   go bad/mad/bankrupt;
   grow tired/old/desperate/fat;
   turn pale/grey/sour/Protestant.
4. – –
5. Mit dem Wort *information* sind folgende Konstruktionen möglich: *She did not give me much information. This is important information. Can you please give me a bit/word/piece of information.*
6. *gymnasium*, (pl.) *gymnasiums* bzw. *gymnasia* = Turnhalle, Sporthalle, *stipend* = Gehalt (bes. von Geistlichen), *his study* = sein Arbeitszimmer, *become* = werden.

Lernphase 2

1. – –
2. – –
3. *Affect* wird sehr häufig als Verb gebraucht und zwar in der Bedeutung von „*cause, change, influence, arouse feelings*". Als Nomen wird es in der Regel nur von Psychologen bzw. bei psychologischen Sachverhalten verwendet im Sinne von „*the emotional side of behaviour*". *Effect* wird normalerweise als Nomen verwendet und zwar in der Bedeutung „*result*". Als Verb wird es nur selten gebraucht. Es ist beschränkt auf sehr formelle Situationen und bedeutet dann „*bring about, cause*".

Beispiele:
affect: Smoking affects health. She was deeply affected by the news of his accident.
effect: Production was halted until repairs could be effected. We have tried our best to effect a reconciliation between the two parties.
4. *I have not finished my studies yet. How are your medical studies progressing?*
5. Die meisten im Sinne von „die Mehrheit" heißt im Englischen *most*.
Beispiele:
Most people work hard in this country. Most children like to play a lot.
Das meiste/am meisten wird in der Regel mit *the most* wiedergegeben.
Beispiele:
He usually talks the most. The most my mother ever earned in one week was eighty pounds.
6. – –
7. Einige typische Kollokationen mit *do* und *make* sind:
do a play/one's military service/a translation/one's hair/a sum/the housework/ homework/the cooking/German/the talking.
make bread/cars/coffee/peace/a journey, journeys/a mistake, mistakes/a plan, plans/money/a remark, remarks.

Übungsphase 1

1. *I have worked/have been working a lot recently/lately/of late.*
2. *My girlfriend visited me recently/not long ago/the other day* („neulich").
3. *How can you/one explain these phenomena?*
4. *Many parents send their children to (a) grammar school.*
5. *The leaves are turning yellow.*
6. *The milk (has) turned sour.*
7. *She wants to become a doctor.*
8. *She became/got very angry with him.*
9. *Many students can only study if they get a grant/scholarship.*
10. *The information in the newspaper was incorrect.*

Übungsphase 2

1. *Many pupils/students are good at French.*
2. *She (has) completed her medical studies successfully.*
3. *Most people can read these days/nowadays.*
4. *I believe everything (that) he said.*
5. *All that glitters is not gold.*
6. *The pupils/students always take their final examinations/finals in (the) summer.*
7. *She is better at physics than (at) Spanish.*
8. *My study is very small.*
9. *I am not surprised that your studies are suffering.*
10. *Will the strike affect the price of coal?*

Text 3

Fehlerkorrektur

1. *on principle/for reasons of principle* 2. *preferable* 3. *less ... than* 4. *such a large choice/so large a choice* 5. *programmes* 6. *the ordinary man* 7. *the ordinary man in the street* 8. *remote control* 9. *particularly high proportion* 10. *harmful to* 11. *who do not notice* 12. *life on the screen/real life* 13. *sensitive children* 14. *often have nightmares* 15. *stage* 16. *it is (to be) feared/we fear* 17. *committee* 18. *take steps*

Lernphase 1

1. Fernbedienung = *remote control*, sensibel = *sensitive*, Stadium = *stage*.
2. – –
3. Endbetonte zweisilbige, auf einen einfachen Konsonanten ausgehende Wörter verdoppeln den Endkonsonaten bei vokalisch anlautender Silbe.
Die aufgeführten Schreibungen *prefers* [prɪˈfɜːz], *preferring* [prɪˈfɜːrɪŋ], *preferred* [prɪˈfɜːd] und *preferable* [ˈpref(ə)rəbl] sind alle korrekt.
4. – –
5. – –
6. Die AE Schreibung ist *program*, während die BE Schreibung *programme* lautet. In der Computersprache findet sich im BE auch die Schreibung *program*. Das Wort Telegramm wird im BE und AE *telegram* geschrieben.
7. *sensible* = vernünftig, *stadium*, (pl.) *stadiums* bzw. *stadia* = Stadion.

Lernphase 2

1. – –
2. Der einfache Mann/die einfache Frau auf der Straße = *the (ordinary) man/the (ordinary) woman in the street* bzw. der einfache Mensch auf der Straße = *the (ordinary) man/the (ordinary) man or woman in the street*, schädlich für = *harmful to*, Schritte unternehmen = *take steps*.
3. *Simple* im Zusammenhang mit Personen wie *man* oder *woman* kann mit „einfach", „schlicht" oder „einfältig" übersetzt werden.
4. – –
5. Bemerken kann u.a. folgendermaßen übersetzt werden:
bemerken (im Sinne von „wahrnehmen") = *notice*
Did you notice anyone leave/leaving the house? I noticed that she was very nervous.
bemerken (im Sinne von „äußern") = *remark*

He remarked that it was getting late. As Stephenson remarked, "To travel hopefully is a better thing than to arrive."
bemerken (im Sinne von „merken") = *realize/-ise*
I did not realize you lived so close. He realized the significance of what she was trying to do.
6. Ohne Artikel stehen im Englischen 1) Abstrakta wie z.b. *art, history, literature, peace* und *science;* 2) Gebäudebezeichnungen im Sinne einer dort üblichen Verrichtung wie z.b. *church, college, prison* und *university;* 3) Kollektiva (Sammelnamen) wie z.b. *mankind, Christendom* (Christenheit), *posterity* und *society;* 4) Stoffnamen (bei allgemeiner Verwendung) wie z.B. *iron, gold, wheat* und *bread;* 5) als einzige Gattungsnamen im Singular *man* und *woman.*
7. – –
8. – –
9. Komitee unterscheidet sich vom englischen Wort *committee* in Schreibung und Aussprache ([kə'mɪtiː]). Dem Wort *committee* kann sowohl das Verb im Singular (formale Kongruenz: „die Gruppe als Einheit") als auch im Plural (Sinnkongruenz: „einzelne Mitglieder einer Gruppe") folgen.
Kommando, Kommerz und Komödie sind im Englischen *commando, commerce* und *comedy.*

Übungsphase 1

1. *I will not take part in the meeting on principle.*
2. *The missile is guided by remote control.*
3. *Gradual change is preferable to sudden change.*
4. *I prefer not to think about it.*
5. *I will earn less money this year than last (year).*
6. *I had not expected such a big crowd/so big a crowd.*
7. *Such lovely weather is rare in England.*
8. *The (ordinary) man in the street cannot understand why the government does/do not take (any) steps to reduce unemployment./The (ordinary) man or woman in the street cannot understand why the government does/do not take (any) steps to reduce unemployment.*
9. *He is a simple man.*

Übungsphase 2

1. *Everyday life can often be boring.*
2. *He often has strange dreams.*
3. *Sensitive people often have very good ideas.*
4. *It is (to be) feared/we fear that he could/might fail at this stage.*
5. *The football stadium was fuller/more crowded than usual.*
6. *"My sister is a great help to me," he remarked.*

7. *This committee is difficult to work with./It is difficult to work with this committee.*
8. *I have not noticed her./I did not notice her.*
9. *This programme may be harmful to children.*

Text 4

Fehlerkorrektur

1. *an educational experiment*   2. *the lives of thousands of people*   3. *doctorates*   4. *devotes itself ... to teaching*   5. *work closely with the BBC*   6. *superior to*   7. *centres/centre*   8. *available to*   9. *receive*   10. *exercises*   11. *addresses*   12. *best sellers*   13. *personal contact*   14. *each student also has the opportunity*   15. *few buildings*   16. *consistently*   17. *who left school*   18. *an MA*   19. *twentieth anniversary*

Lernphase 1

1. Promotion (Doktorprüfung) = *doctorate* bzw. *PhD*, konsequent (im Sinne von „beharrlich") = *persistent*, (im Sinne von „folgerichtig") = *consistent*, (im Sinne von „streng, hart") = *rigorous*.
2. – –
3. – –
4. Nach *devote* steht folgende verbale Konstruktion: *devote oneself to doing something*.
   Beispiele:
   They have devoted all their time to helping the sick. She has devoted her life to earning more and more money.
5. – –
6. Andere Beispiele sind u.a. *inferior to, senior to, junior to, prior to*.
7. AE *color, traveled/traveling* und *defense* werden im BE *colour, travelled/travelling* und *defence* geschrieben.
8. *Our advanced technology is available to all students.*

Lernphase 2

1. *promotion* = Beförderung, Förderung, Werbekampagne, *consequent* = folgend, sich ergebend, logisch, *consequently* = folglich.
2. Die korrekten Schreibungen lauten *receive, exercises, addresses, best sellers* (AE auch *best-sellers*). Bei den falschen Schreibungen von *addresses* und *best sellers*

liegt wahrscheinlich Interferenz durch das Deutsche vor, während die falsche Schreibung von *exercises* möglicherweise auf Interferenz des französischen Wortes beruht. Die falsche Schreibung von *receive* basiert entweder auf Intraferenz (siehe *believe, thieves* u.ä.) oder auf Interferenz durch das Deutsche.
3. Siehe Lösung zu Text 3, Lernphase 2, Nummer 6.
4. Als allgemeine Regel gilt, daß Adverbien entweder vor dem Verb, zwischen Hilfsverb und Verb oder zwischen *be* und Adjektiv stehen: *She always reads at night. He has always read at night. He is always sleepy.* (Siehe auch Text 3, Lernphase 2, Nummer 7 im Textteil.)
5. *A few buildings* bzw. *a few friends* kann übersetzt werden mit „einige/ein paar Häuser/Freunde". *Few buildings* bzw. *few friends* sind „wenige Gebäude" bzw. „wenige Freunde".
6. Siehe zunächst Lösung zu Text 3, Lernphase 2, Nummer 6. Die allgemeine Regel lautet, daß Gebäudebezeichnungen im Sinne einer dort üblichen Verrichtung ohne den Artikel stehen: *I go to school.* Bei konkreter Bedeutung im Sinne eines bestimmten Gebäudes steht der Artikel: *The school I go to is old.*
Abweichend von der ersten Regel finden sich u.a. neben *in hospital* auch *in the hospital* (AE) und neben *at university* auch *at the university* (BE, AE).
7. Entscheidend für den Gebrauch von *a* und *an* ist die Aussprache des Anlauts des folgenden Wortes. Bei vokalischer Aussprache steht *an* (z.B. *an MP* [ənˌem'piː], *an MA* [ənˌem'eɪ], *an MCP* [ənˌemsiː'piː] und *an only child* [ənˌəʊnlɪ'tʃaɪld]), bei konsonantischer Aussprache (auch [j] und [w]) immer ein *a* (z.B. *a one-man show* [əˌwʌnmæn'ʃəʊ] und *a European* [əjʊərə'piːən]).
8. birthday: *Happy birthday! It's my birthday today. For her hundredth birthday I bought her an electric blanket.*
anniversary: *We celebrated our wedding anniversary in Paris. It's the twentieth anniversary of our country's independence. It's the hundredth anniversary of the composer's death.*

Übungsphase 1

1. *The wealth of a nation often depends on its level of education.*
2. *In this region, the lives of many people are threatened by air pollution.*
3. *It was also his wedding anniversary.*
4. *She received a lot of cards for her 18th birthday.*
5. *After the state's 40th anniversary celebrations had taken place, a peaceful revolution swept through the country.*
6. *A doctorate is the prerequisite for a successful career in chemistry.*
7. *She took a computing course to improve her chances of promotion.*
8. *I think you have to be persistent if you want to achieve a certain goal.*
9. *He is a consistent supporter of penal reform.*
10. *We will take rigorous action.*

11. She devoted her life to helping blind people.
12. There are good chances of promotion in this firm.
13. The bank did not lend him any money. Consequently, he went bankrupt.
14. She writes one best seller/best-seller (AE) a year.

Übungsphase 2

1. Don't come too close!
2. She examined the photographs very closely.
3. The computer is vastly superior to the book.
4. Where is the town centre?
5. We want to make our products available to a wider market.
6. You will receive a list of best sellers from your bookshop.
7. Look at Exercise 18 in your book.
8. I cannot read the address on this envelope.
9. At that point radio contact was broken.
10. Personal contact is very important in this firm.
11. At this university, every student can get a BA and an MA in history.
12. The town also has a few old buildings.
13. Only few buildings were destroyed during the war.
14. I hated school.

Text 5

Fehlerkorrektur

1. *These days*   2. *to rise*   3. *has used his imagination*   4. *to cast a shadow over*
5. *space*   6. *his theory is that/it is estimated that*   7. *four hundred billion pounds*
8. *it would take twenty years*   9. *to be sceptical*   10. *this is after all*

Lernphase 1

1. Phantasie = *imagination* („Einbildungskraft"), *fantasy* („Trugbild, Einbildung", pl. „Phantasievorstellungen").
   imagination: The story shows plenty of imagination. He has got a vivid imagination.
   fantasy: The whole story was a fantasy. Let's talk about Jane's fantasies about a voyage up the Nile.

2. – –
3. *fly* (tr.) – *fly* (intr.): *The pilot flew the plane to London. – The damaged aircraft was flying on only one engine.*
work (tr.) – *work* (intr.): *They work us too hard in this office. – I work in a factory.*
raise (tr.) – *rise* (intr.): *The king raised an army. – Smoke rose from the factory chimneys.*
lay (tr.) – *lie* (intr.): *They laid the injured person on the grass. – They just lie on the beach all day.*
fell (tr.) – *fall* (intr.): *The blow would have felled most men. – He fell off the ladder.*
4. *shade:* Schatten („schattiges Plätzchen, Kühle spendender, schattiger Platz"): *I am too hot in the sun. Let's go into the shade. They were sitting in the shade of the tree.*
shadow: Schatten („scharf umrissener Schatten, der von jdm./etwas geworfen wird"): *Shadows are longer when the sun is low in the sky. The chair casts a shadow on the wall.*
5. – –
6. – –

Lernphase 2

1. – –
2. *Take* kann mit „dauern" im Sinne von „benötigen, brauchen" übersetzt werden: *It takes ten hours to fly to New York.*
last heißt u.a. „dauern" im Sinne von „andauern, anhalten": *The hot weather lasted until October.*
3. *It would last twenty years* heißt im Deutschen „Es würde zwanzig Jahre halten/so bleiben/reichen/andauern".
4. *Sceptic* (AE *skeptic*) heißt im Deutschen „Skeptiker".
5. *Sceptic* ['skeptɪk] heißt „Skeptiker" und *septic* ['septɪk] heißt „septisch, vereitert".
6. *eventually:* schließlich, endlich, sich (als Folge) ergebend: *She worked so hard that eventually she made herself ill. After many attempts she eventually managed to get a promotion.*
finally: schließlich, endlich, zum Schluß, zuletzt, letztlich: *After several delays, the plane finally left at 7 o'clock. And finally, I would just like to say this.*
at last: endlich, schließlich, zuletzt: *At last we found out what had really happened. He's here, at last.*
after all: nach allem, immerhin, schließlich (im Sinne von „trotzdem"): *So you see I was right after all. I know they haven't finished the work, but, after all, they are very busy.*
Finally und *at last* haben die Grundbedeutung von „zuletzt", *eventually* hat die Grundbedeutung von „schließlich noch", und *after all* bedeutet vor allem „immerhin".

Übungsphase 1

1. These days, people don't eat as much meat as they used to.
2. The sun rises in the east.
3. She raised her hand.
4. He lives in a world of fantasy.
5. She has a vivid imagination.
6. I am too hot in the sun. Let's get into the shade.
7. As it grew dark, the shadows grew longer/lengthened.
8. The space between the two cars was too narrow.
9. The satellite had been in space for two years.

Übungsphase 2

1. She said that she would come early.
2. Is it true that you are getting marrried?
3. It takes forty hours to build this car.
4. His bad mood won't last.
5. Everyone says that our team will win, but I am sceptical.
6. The sceptic will argue against this plan.
7. I know that he hasn't finished the work, but, after all, he's very busy.
8. The pound has fallen again.

Text 6

Hinweis: Diejenigen Sätze, die im formellen BE verfaßt und mit dem AE identisch sind, werden nicht besonders gekennzeichnet.

Übungsphase 1

1. It is the house of which the roof is damaged. It is the house the roof of which is damaged. It is the house whose roof is damaged. (infml.)
2. A nurse has many duties to fulfil. A nurse has many duties to fulfill. (AE)
3. Today's public is not interested in this issue. Today's public are not interested in this issue. (infml.)
4. This time, you have made fewer mistakes than last time. This time, you have made less mistakes than last time. (infml.)
5. Jane is not as tall as Margaret. Jane is not so tall as Margaret.
6. Everybody thinks he has a right to stay. Everybody thinks they have a right to stay. (infml.) Everybody thinks he or she has a right to stay.

7. *I will communicate my views orally to the members of the committee. I will communicate my views verbally to the members of the committee.*
8. *Mary and Joan are quite different from each other. Mary and Joan are quite different to each other. Mary and Joan are quite different than each other.* (AE)
9. *It is hoped that the students in this tutorial will pass the final test. I hope that the students in this tutorial will pass the final test. The students in this tutorial will hopefully pass the final test.* (infml.)
10. *Many a student does not realize that he has to work hard for examinations. Many a student does not realize that he or she has (got) to work hard for exams.* (infml.)

Übungsphase 2

1. *Berlin's most famous monuments are situated in the centre of the town.*
2. *The museum's treasures can be viewed/are on view for the first time.*
3. *She spoke loudly and clearly. She spoke loud and clear.*
4. *They missed the ferry owing to the snow. They missed the ferry because of the snow. They missed the ferry due to the snow.*
5. *I want to drive quickly to Boot's/Boots' to pick up my prescription. I want to quickly drive to Boots to pick up my prescription.* (infml.) (*To Boot's/Boots'* ist heutzutage im BE akzeptabel im formellen Stil, nicht aber *to Boots* = infml., s. auch Text 9, Übungsphase 1, Nr. 7 im Lösungsteil.)
6. *I do not dare to contradict. I do not dare contradict.* (infml.) *I dare not contradict.*
7. *You do not need to follow her advice. You do not need follow her advice.* (infml.) *You need not follow her advice.*
8. *The group's spokesman was extremely intelligent. The group's spokeswoman was extremely intelligent. The group's spokesperson was extremely intelligent.*
9. *I won't accept your offer under any circumstances. No way will I accept your offer.* (infml.)

Text 7

Fehlerkorrektur

1. *boasts the busiest roads*   2. *busiest roads in the world*   3. *forty*   4. *will be halved*   5. *solutions to this problem*   6. *to be spent on*   7. *enthusiasts are pinning their hopes*   8. *new technology*   9. *being equipped*   10. *advice*   11. *advice on*   12. *braking the car*   13. *a couple of drinks too many*   14. *prevented (from) driving*   15. *out of the driver's hands*

Lernphase 1

1. Technik = *technology* („Technologie, Technik als Leistung der Zivilisation"), *technique* („Methode, Verfahren, Technik").
   technology: The system uses advanced computer technology. Our belief in the power of modern technology has been shaken.
   technique: They have developed a very sophisticated welding technique. She displayed a flawless technique.
2. *boast sth.* = sich rühmen, stolz sein auf – *boast of/about sth.* = prahlen.
   Boast sth. drückt also eine neutrale oder positive Haltung aus, während *boast of/about sth.* eher eine negative Eigenschaft beschreibt.
3. Häufige Kollokationen mit *world* sind u.a. *all over the world, the whole world, worlds apart* und *on top of the world*.
   Nach superlativischem Adjektiv steht immer *in the world* (Der reichste Mann der Welt = *the richest man in the world*).
4. *four, fourteen, forty*
5. – –
6. typisch für = *typical of,* charakteristisch für = *characteristic of,* gelten für = *true of/for,* ausgeben für = *spend on,* Lösung für (ein Problem) = *solution to (a problem),* Symbol für = *symbol of/for,* Beispiel für etwas/jn. = *example of sth./to sb.*, Zeichen für = *sign of,* Grund für = *reason for,* Beweis für = *proof of.*

Achtung: In den Texten einiger britischer Linguisten wie Quirk, Crystal, Halliday etc. finden sich sehr vereinzelt auch *?typical for* und *?characteristic for.* Hier scheint eine Entwicklung im Gang zu sein, die am Ende in einigen der obigen Fälle neben der Präpositon *of* möglicherweise auch die Variante mit *for* zulassen wird. Diese Tendenz ist aber in den einschlägigen Grammatiken und Wörterbücher noch nicht kodifiziert. In den einsprachigen Wörterbüchern wie in dem **Collins COBUILD English Language Dictionary** (1987), **Dictionary of Contempory English** (1987) und dem **Oxford Advanced Learner's Dictionary** (1989) finden sich jedenfalls noch keine derartigen Hinweise. Allerdings sollte man den oben genannten Fällen besondere Beachtung schenken, da sich hier eventuell eine Entwicklung anbahnt (s. Appendix).

Lernphase 2

1. Gegenteilige Beispiele sind *We are keeping an open mind, They vented their spleen on him* und *They can't put their finger on what's wrong.*
2. Die Regel heißt, daß einfache, betonte Endkonsonanten vor vokalisch anlautender Endung verdoppelt werden. Es gibt aber auch Ausnahmen wie z.B. *travelled, worshipped* und *handicapped.*
   Die Vergangenheitsformen lauten *preferred, regretted, developed, travelled, worshipped* und *panicked.*
3. *A piece of advice on how to do something.*

4. *Brake the car* heißt „den Wagen bremsen" und *break the car* „das Auto (Spielzeugauto) kaputtmachen".
5. *The centre forward has pulled a muscle. He has just played one game too many. Don't pay any attention to him – he's had one too many.*
6. *Unless we get more funding, we'll be prevented (from) finishing our experimental programme. My only idea was to prevent him (from) speaking.*
7. Der Unterschied besteht darin, daß mit *hand* natürlich nur eine Hand gemeint ist, während sich *hands* auf beide Hände bezieht. Im Text 7 ist *hands* angemessener, weil *hands* immer dann gebraucht wird, wenn eine Kontrollfunktion gemeint ist.

Übungsphase 1

1. *Our street boasts the oldest houses in the town.*
2. *He is always boasting about his children.*
3. *She is the richest woman in the world.*
4. *I'll be forty-four next year.*
5. *She tried to halve the costs of the project.*
6. *There are no simple solutions to the unemployment problem.*
7. *What did you spend the money on?*
8. *They pinned their hopes on the new government.*
9. *If you want to learn to paint, I suggest you study Turner's technique.*
10. *This printing plant uses the most modern technology.*

Übungsphase 2

1. *This is one of the well-equipped hospitals.*
2. *Can I give you a piece of advice?*
3. *They want (to have) some advice on how to master the situation.*
4. *Be careful when you brake! You might stall the engine.*
5. *Father to son: "Don't break the car!"*
6. *He had had one drink too many.*
7. *They were prevented (from) demonstrating in the street.*
8. *She took the child by the hand.*
9. *The lovers stood in front of the shop holding hands.*

Text 8

Fehlerkorrektur

1. *what weather/such weather*   2. *set foot in*   3. *go on complaining*   4. *have noticed*   5. *are used to living*   6. *learn from archaeologists*   7. *threat to ancient Britons*   8. *dozens of animals*   9. *proof of*   10. *to take advantage of*   11. *most of them*

Lernphase 1

1. – –
2. *She lived in Paris for years without ever setting foot in the Louvre. He was the first man to set foot on the moon.*
3. *Go on complaining* heißt im Deutschen „sich weiterhin beklagen" oder „fortfahren, sich zu beklagen", hingegen wird *she/he went on to complain* mit „und dann beklagte sie/er sich" übersetzt. *He went on to say* heißt also „dann sagte er".
4. – –
5. Auf *used to* folgt ein Infinitiv, während nach *be used to* und *get used to* die Konstruktion Verb + *-ing* steht.
   used to do sth. = früher mal etwas getan haben: *I used to go fishing.*
   be used to doing sth. = gewohnt sein, etwas zu tun: *I am used to working a lot.*
   get used to doing sth. = sich daran gewöhnen, etwas zu tun: *She is getting used to working a lot.*
6. Das Englische *learn of/about sth.* heißt im Deutschen „erfahren, hören von" (= *become aware of sth. through information or observation/realize*). *Learn from sb./sth.* kann mit „von jemanden/aus einer Sache lernen" (= *gain knowledge or skill by study, experience being taught*) übersetzt werden.
   Beispiele:
   learn of/about: I am sorry to learn of/about your illness. They offered help as soon as they learnt of/about the accident.
   learn from: He has learnt from his mistakes. What can we learn from this woman?

Lernphase 2

1. *Threat of* heißt im Deutschen „Bedrohung von" (= *a sign, warning, or possibility of coming danger*), *threat to* bedeutet „Gefahr für" (= *a person, thing, or idea regarded as a possible danger*).
   Beispiele:
   threat of: The clouds brought a threat of rain. The threat of bancruptcy hung over the company.

threat to: While the killer goes free he is a threat to everyone in the town. Some people see computers as a threat to their jobs.
2. – –
3. *Proof of* ist im Deutschen „Beweis(e) für". Im Englischen steht *proof* in dieser Bedeutung in der Regel im Singular. *Proof* bedeutet weiterhin „Probe" und „Alkoholgehalt". Außerdem heißt *proof/proofs* auch „Korrekturfahne(n)" und „Probeabzug/Probeabzüge".
4. Etwas ausnutzen heißt im Englischen *take advantage of.*
   Beispiele:
   You should take advantage of the fine weather. She took full advantage of the hotel's facilities.
5. – –

Übungsphase 1

1. *What awful weather!*
2. *They were the first to set foot on the island.*
3. *They were the first to set foot out of the door.*
4. *They were the first Europeans to set foot in America.*
5. *They went on complaining despite the good economic situation.*
6. *She interrupted her speech and went on to complain about the carelessness of industry.*
7. *"A good idea", she remarked.*
8. *She noticed that she had forgotten her keys.*
9. *We used to live in London.*
10. *They are used to having guests.*
11. *We are getting used to having guests.*

Übungsphase 2

1. *He never seems to learn from his mistakes.*
2. *We learnt about/of our daughter's marriage on the way to Paris.*
3. *Air pollution is a threat to the whole of mankind/humankind.*
4. *There was a threat of rain.*
5. *There were dozens of attempts at school reform.*
6. *Have you (got) any proof of his guilt?*
7. *I received the proofs yesterday.*
8. *You should take advantage of the fine weather.*
9. *Most people take their holidays in (the) summer.*

Text 9

Hinweis: Diejenigen Sätze, die im formellen BE verfaßt und mit dem AE identisch sind, werden nicht besonders gekennzeichnet.

Übungsphase 1

1. *My aim in life is to be successful. My life's aim is to be successful.*
2. *I ate (my) lunch after Jane had come back from shopping. I ate (my) lunch after Jane came back from shopping.*
3. *It was not too hot. It wasn't too hot.* (infml.)
4. *We all had flu. We all had the flu.*
5. *I still had to go to the hairdresser's. I still had to go to the hairdresser.* (infml.)
6. *You had better stay at home. You better stay at home.* (infml.)
7. *I have an account at Barclay's. I have an account at Barclays'. I have (got) an account at Barclays.* (infml.)

Übungsphase 2

1. *As far as the weather was concerned, last summer was fantastic. Weatherwise, last summer was fantastic.* (infml. BE, AE)
2. *Harrod's has sold more china this year than last (year). Harrods has sold more china this year than last (year).* (infml.) *Harrods have sold more china this year than last (year).*
3. *She then felt (that) she had to do something. She now felt (that) she had to do something.*
4. *It took me half an hour to get to the station. It took me a half hour to get to the station.* (BE rare, AE)
5. *She had passed her exam and went home happy. She had passed her exam and went home happily. She had passed her exam and happily went home.*
6. *The woman entered the hotel, rather self-confident. The woman entered the hotel rather self-confidently.* (Die beiden Sätze sind in ihrer Bedeutung ein wenig verschieden!)
7. *I am looking forward to a five day stay in Berlin. I am looking forward to a five-day stay in Berlin. I am looking forward to a five days stay in Berlin. I am looking forward to a five days' stay in Berlin.*
8. *If I were an actor, I would only play serious parts. If I was an actor, I would only play serious parts. (infml.)*

Text 10

Fehlerkorrektur

1. *environmental pollution/stop pollution*   2. *looks grim*   3. *factories*   4. *what the earth will look like/how the earth will look*   5. *a single tree*   6. *keep on worrying*   7. *environmentally friendly/environment friendly*   8. *to put it in*   9. *car engine*   10. *comically*   11. *ourselves*   12. *nourished on*   13. *they will no longer be*   14. *allergic to*   15. *they are evolving lungs*   16. *tragic*

Lernphase 1

1. Fabrik = *factory* (allg. Bezeichnung), *mill* (Papier-, Stahl-, Baumwollfabrik), *plant* (Produktionsanlage, Werk); Motor = *engine* (vom Auto, Flugzeug); Lunge = *lungs*.
   Beispiele:
   factory: He works in a car factory.
   mill: Paper is made in a paper mill.
   plant: They have just built a new chemical plant.
   engine: This car needs a new engine.
   lungs: Smoking is bad for your lungs.
2. – –
3. – –
4. – –
5. Das deutsche Wort einzeln kann im Englischen u.a. mit *individual* („eigen", „individuell", „separat"), *single* („einzig, Einzel-") und *solitary* („alleinstehend", „einzig") wiedergegeben werden.
   Beispiele:
   individual: Each individual leaf on the tree is different. Review committees consider the cases of individual prisoners.
   single: We heard a single shot. We went there every single day.
   solitary: I remember that solitary ash tree by the lake. Can you give me one solitary piece of proof for what you say?
6. – –
7. – –
8. – –

Lernphase 2

1. – –
2. *We keep ourselves fit* bzw. *we keep fit* heißt „wir halten uns (selbst) fit", während *they keep us fit* mit „sie halten uns (also andere) fit" übersetzt wird. Im ersten Fall

liegt eine echte Rückbeziehung (Reflexivität) vor, d.h. die Handlung wird vom Subjekt an sich selber vollzogen. Das zusammengesetzte Pronomen mit -*self* ist im obigen Fall fakultativ. Im zweiten Fall liegt keine Rückbeziehung vor, deshalb steht ein einfaches Personalpronomen.
3. – –
4. In der Regel wird <u>nicht mehr</u> im Englischen mit *no longer* bzw. *any longer* übersetzt, wenn die Aussage rein zeitlich gemeint ist, hingegen steht *no more* bzw. *any more*, wenn eine quantitative/qualitative Aussage gemacht wird, die auch den zeitlichen Aspekt miteinbeziehen kann.
Beispiele:
no longer/any longer: She no longer lives here. I used to smoke 40 cigarettes a day, but not any longer!
no more/any more: No more cake for me, thank you! They used to be good friends, but they don't like each other any more.
5. <u>Allergisch gegen</u> heißt im Englischen *allergic to*.
6. *Lungs* heißt „die Lunge", und *lung* bedeutet „(ein) Lungenflügel". In Komposita findet man auch die Form ohne *s* wie beispielsweise *lung cancer*.
7. – –
8. *Fabric* = Stoff(struktur) von Textilien, Gebäudestruktur, Gesellschaftsstruktur, *motor* = bes. Elektromotor, Auto (infml).
fabric: These fabrics are specially imported from Spain and Italy. The entire fabric of the church needs renovation.
motor: This lawn mower is driven by a small electric motor. Where did you buy your motor?
<u>Stoff</u> (im Sinne von „Textil") wird normalerweise mit *material* übersetzt wie in *She bought a few metres of dress material* und *What nice material!*

Übungsphase 1

1. *She looked happy.*
2. *He looked at his daughter happily.*
3. *This fabric is made of nylon and wool.*
4. *Now we know what the surface of the moon looks like. Now we know how the surface of the moon looks.*
5. *Environmental pollution has now reached the North Pole.*
6. *She is an only child.*
7. *A single tree stood in the desert. A solitary tree stood in the desert.*
8. *This product is environmentally/ecologically friendly/beneficial. This product is environment friendly.*
9. *His lungs were healthy.*

Übungsphase 2

1. *She put the book in her briefcase.*
2. *The car engine was broken.*
3. *She wore clothes that were almost comically inappropriate.*
4. *Our young daughter keeps us fit.*
5. *He keeps (himself) fit by jogging a lot.*
6. *Many animals nourish themselves/feed on plants.*
7. *I don't drink beer any longer. I don't drink beer any more. I no longer drink beer.*
(= „Ich habe überhaupt aufgehört, Bier zu trinken.")
I can't/won't drink any more beer. (= „Ich habe schon viel Bier getrunken und kann jetzt kein Bier mehr trinken.")
8. *I am allergic to all kinds of pollen.*
9. *His case was tragic.*
10. *She kept on asking questions.*

Text 11

Fehlerkorrektur

1. *customs barriers*   2. *changes are to be expected*   3. *at the moment*   4. *ideally speaking*   5. *at least three languages/to learn at least one foreign language*   6. *business*   7. *reasons for*   8. *economic*   9. *competition*   10. *vital to them*   11. *all over Britain*   12. *its teaching load*   13. *to lose touch*   14. *in other words*   15. *a Europeanised form*   16. *restricted to rural areas*   17. *others maintain/believe/feel*

Lernphase 1

1. meinen (im Sinne von „behaupten") = *maintain*, Konkurrenz = *competition, mean* (v.) = bedeuten, beabsichtigen, *concurrence* = Zusammentreffen.
   Beispiele:
   maintain: Throughout his trial he maintained his innocence.
   competition: There was intense competition among the journalists to get the story.
   mean: What does it mean? I meant to tell you about it.
   concurrence: What an interesting concurrence of events.
2. – –
3. In dem Fall *Changes are difficult to bring about* steht als Attribut immer der aktive Infinitiv nach prädikativ gebrauchten Adjektiven wie *difficult, easy, fit, good, hard, nice, pleasant* und *ready.*

Beispiele:
This place is easy to reach.
The question was hard to answer.
In dem Fall *changes are to be brought about* muß der passivische Infinitiv stehen. Abweichend vom Deutschen erfolgt eine passivische Infinitivkonstruktion nach den Verben *be, leave* und *remain*.
Beispiele:
Her behaviour leaves much to be desired.
This remains to be seen.
He was not to be found anywhere.
4. – –
5. – –
6. *At last* bedeutet „endlich, schließlich, zuletzt", *at least* heißt „mindestens, wenigstens".
7. *A lot of business* heißt viel Geschäft (im Sinne von „Verdienst", „Arbeit", „Kundschaft"). In dieser Bedeutung ist *business* nicht zählbar (non-count). *Lots of businesses* heißt „viele Läden/Geschäfte/Firmen". In dieser Bedeutung ist *business* zählbar (count).
8. – –

Lernphase 2

1. *Economic* heißt „nationalökonomisch, (volks)wirtschaftlich", *economical* kann mit „sparsam" oder „haushälterisch" übersetzt werden.
2. – –
3. – –
4. *it's: It's raining. It's too small for me.*
   its: The plan has its merits. The creature lifted its head.
5. [ðə 'bʌtn ɪz 'luːs], [aɪ 'heɪt tə 'luːz 'bʌtnz], ['kæn jʊ 'pliːz 'luːsn ðə 'bʌtnz]
6. – –
7. – –
8. – –

Übungsphase 1

1. *Some customs barriers have fallen in Europe in the past years.*
2. *Many changes are to be expected in Eastern Europe.*
3. *Ideally speaking, every European should speak at least two languages.*
4. *You can do business with us.*
5. *He runs several small businesses/shops.*
6. *The reason for his behaviour was not clear.*
7. *They did it for economic reasons.*
8. *This method of heating is very economical.*

9. There is a lot of competition from abroad.
10. What an interesting concurrence of events.

Übungsphase 2

1. It is vital to animals to obey their instincts.
2. Everywhere in Europe/all over Europe/in the whole of Europe, people are talking about the end of the Cold War.
3. It's his idea.
4. This is the most recent computer. Its performance is unbeatable.
5. He did not want to lose his patience.
6. Two buttons were loose.
7. In other words, he was just too lazy to learn the rules.
8. At last we found out what had really happened that night.
9. There will soon be a European passport.
10. Many people maintain that this illness is restricted to one section of the population.

Text 12

Fehlerkorrektur

1. *logical deduction*   2. *some people*   3. *novels*   4. *altogether*   5. *nineteen plays; West End play; longest-running play*   6. *she was born*   7. *when she was a child*   8. *first marriage*   9. *marriage to Archibald*   10. *her husband's involvement; her husband's lover*   11. *suffered from amnesia*   12. *who was an archaeologist*   13. *the couple*   14. *travelled*   15. *the setting for*   16. *the setting for many of her plots*   17. *her grandson now runs/heads the firm*   18. *her literary agent*   19. *her work*   20. *on television*   21. *nostalgia*   22. *the elegant atmosphere*   23. *the good old days*   24. *testifies to her poularity*

Lernphase 1

1. logisch = *logical*, Roman = *novel*, Stück (im Sinne von „Theaterstück") = *play*, ein Paar = *couple* (= „Ehepaar", „zwei Personen") und *a pair* (= zwei Dinge wie z.B. ein Paar Schuhe), mondän = *fashionable, elegant, chic*.
   Beispiele:
   logical: I made little attempt at logical argument.
   novel: He has written ten novels.
   play: The drama society are going to put on a play.

couple: The young couple decided to leave their village.
pair: He bought three pairs of shoes.
fashionable: He moves in fashionable circles.
2. Der Plural von *person* ist normalerweise *people*. Die Form *persons* ist sehr formell und wird meist in offiziellen Kontexten verwendet wie z.B. in dem Satz *He is accused of conspiring with person or persons unknown.*
3. − −
4. − −
5. − −
6. *wedding* = Trauung, Hochzeit (Zeremonie), Vermählung (Zeremonie), *marriage* = Ehe, Hochzeit mit (*to*)
Meine Heirat mit John heißt im Englischen *My marriage to John.*
7. *My man* für „mein Ehemann" ist sehr informell und entspricht ungefähr dem Deutschen „mein Alter".
8. Leiden unter einer Krankheit heißt im Englischen *suffer from a disease.*
9. Ich bin Student ist im Englischen *I am a student.* Abweichend vom Deutschen wird im Englischen der unbestimmte Artikel verwendet, wenn eine Person als Vertreter einer speziellen Gruppe (z.B. Berufsgruppe, Nationalität, Religionsgemeinschaft, Partei) charakterisiert wird.
10. Die Schreibung *travelled* ist BE, hingegen ist *traveled* im AE üblich.

Lernphase 2

1. *logic* = Logik, *roman* = Antiqua(schrift), *Roman* = römisch, Römer(in), *mundane* = schlicht und einfach, weltlich, profan.
logic: We have to accept the logic of his argument.
roman: The words in the definition are set in roman type.
Roman: This is an old Roman road.
mundane: I lead a pretty mundane life; nothing interesting ever happens to me.
2. − −
3. − −
4. − −
5. − −
6. − −
7. − −
8. − −
9. − −
10. *As* als Konjunktion kann u.a. mit „wie", „während" oder „als" (bei Gleichzeitigkeit), „weil" oder „da" und „obwohl" übersetzt werden.
Beispiele:
As I said in my last letter, I am taking the exam in June.
He saw him as she was getting off the bus.
As he has no car, she can't get there easily.
Tired as I was, I tried to help him.

Übungsphase 1

1. *It is only logical that we must do something about environmental pollution.*
2. *All the people present were arrested.*
3. *I cannot follow his logic.*
4. *She wrote twelve novels.*
5. *The Romans occupied the whole of England/all of England.*
6. *This column is printed in roman type.*
7. *He played in fourteen test matches altogether.*
8. *She has written a new play.*
9. *Things were different when I was a child.*

Übungsphase 2

1. *I was born in London.*
2. *I travelled a lot when I was young.* (BE) *I traveled a lot when I was young.* (AE)
3. *There were a lot of guests at the wedding.*
4. *Her family disapproved of her marriage to John.*
5. *Her husband's reputation was excellent.*
6. *I sometimes suffer from headache(s).*
7. *My friend is an archaeologist.*
8. *They are a nice couple.*
9. *I have bought (myself) a pair of new shoes.*
10. *The setting for his plots was always Africa.*

Übungsphase 3

1. *They run a small hotel.*
2. *Who is her literary agent?*
3. *Shakespeare's works will never lose their popularity.*
4. *I have finished my homework.*
5. *Where is the gas works?*
6. *Did you see the Prime Minister on television last night?*
7. *I cannot understand many people's nostalgia for the so-called good old days.*
8. *This place is very chic/elegant/fashionable.*
9. *He led a very mundane existence.*
10. *Her nervous behaviour testified to her guilt.*
11. *Nostalgia can be seen as a significant phenomenon of this decade.*

Text 13

Fehlerkorrektur

1. *recent report*   2. *example of*   3. *male and female behaviour*   4. *girls use pain killers*   5. *fourteen*   6. *society expects girls to be slim*   7. *by the time they are fifteen*   8. *two-thirds have dieted/been on a diet/gone on a diet*   9. *junk food like/such as fizzy drinks*   10. *quite different*   11. *girls brush their teeth*   12. *boys spend a lot of time*   13. *watching television*   14. *girls devote their time to doing work for school or going*   15. *discos*   16. *girls do more homework/to do homework*   17. *who have stopped doing*   18. *e.g./eg*   19. *girls get used to drinking alcohol and smoking*   20. *boy-friend/boyfriend*   21. *in the near future*

Lernphase 1

1. Das deutsche Wort *aktuell* kann u.a. mit *current* (Problem, Entwicklung), *present* (Problem, Zeit), *topical* (Buch, Film, Thema) und *latest* (Mode) übersetzt werden.
   Beispiele:
   current: I have closely followed the current events in India.
   present: Our present problems can be solved quite easily.
   topical: It is a play full of topical allusions to well-known people.
   latest: They showed the latest fashions from Paris.
2. Das englische Wort *actual* heißt im Deutschen „eigentlich, tatsächlich". *Actually* kann mit „übrigens", „eigentlich" und „tatsächlich" übersetzt werden.
3. – –
4. *male* = männlich („von männlichem Geschlecht"), *masculine* = männlich, maskulin (im Sinne von sogenannten „typisch männlichen Eigenschaften"), *manly* = männlich, mannhaft.
   male: The male voice is deeper than the female voice.
   masculine: She looks rather masculine in that suit.
   manly: The boy walked with a confident, manly stride.
5. *female* = weiblich („von weiblichem Geschlecht", *male* ist das Gegenteil), *feminine* = weiblich, fraulich (im Sinne von sogenannten „typisch weiblichen Eigenschaften", *masculine* ist das Gegenteil), *womanly* = fraulich, sehr weiblich (*manly* ist das Gegenteil), *effeminate* = weibisch, weichlich, verweichlicht.
   female: The male fertilizes the female's eggs.
   feminine: She dresses in a very feminine way.
   womanly: She showed a womanly concern for her health.
   effeminate: They find European males slightly effeminate.
6. – –

7. Die korrekten Schreibungen lauten *fourteen, quite* und *boy-friend/boyfriend*.
8. Im Englischen steht nach erwarten, daß ... bei verschiedenen Subjekten in Haupt- und Nebensatz eine Objekt + Infinitivkonstruktion mit *to* (der sog. A.c.I.). D.h., das Subjekt des Nebensatzes wird zum direkten Objekt in einer Infinitivkonstruktion mit *to*. Der Satz Ich erwarte, daß sie ihre Pflicht tut heißt im Englischen *I expect her to do her duty.*

Lernphase 2

1. – –
2. *Until* und *till* sind bedeutungsgleich und können mit „bis (zu einem Zeitpunkt hin)" übersetzt werden. *Until* ist etwas formeller als *till*. *By* bedeutet „bis (spätestens)".
Beispiele:
until/till: Let's wait until/till the rain stops. I waited until 10 o'clock.
by: Be here by 6 o'clock. Will you finish it by tomorrow?
3. – –
4. Wie (zum Beispiel) kann im Englischen entweder mit *like (for example)* oder *such as* übersetzt werden.
Beispiele:
like: You only find them in big countries like Brazil and India. Practical lessons, like woodwork and cookery, are not considered as important as maths.
such as: We have planted lots of flowers such as roses, carnations, and daffodils. Countries such as France, Britain and Italy have similar political systems.
5. – –
6. – –
7. – –

Lernphase 3

1. – –
2. Nach *devote to* erfolgt die Konstruktion Verb + *-ing* wie beispielsweise *He devoted all his efforts to fighting against pollution.*
3. Die Pluralformen lauten *grotto(e)s, ghetto(e)s, studios, radios, echoes, potatoes, vetoes, cargo(e)s* und *volcano(e)s*.
Die Pluralbildung von Wörtern mit der Endung *-o* geschieht mit Hilfe eines Plural *-s* oder *-es*. Der Plural jedes Wortes muß in der Regel einzeln gelernt werden.
Folgende Wörter bilden den Plural auf *-s* (auf alle Fälle gehören hierzu Wörter, denen vor dem finalen *-o* bereits ein Vokal vorangeht): *kilos, radios, casinos, studios, discos, embryos, zoos, photos.*
Folgende Wörter bilden den Plural auf *-es*: *potatoes, tomatoes, Negroes, heroes, echoes, vetoes, embargoes.*
Es gibt auch eine Anzahl von Wörtern, bei denen der Plural sowohl mit *-s* als auch mit *-es* gebildet werden darf: *cargo(e)s, motto(e)s, tornado(e)s, volcano(e)s, grotto(e)s, banjo(e)s.*

4. Hausarbeiten heißt im Englischen *homework*.
5. *I stopped to drink wine* bedeutet soviel wie „Ich hörte mit einer Tätigkeit auf/blieb stehen, um dann Wein zu trinken", während *I stopped drinking wine* im Deutschen „Ich hörte mit dem Weintrinken auf" heißt.
6. – –
7. Nach *get used to* steht die Konstruktion Verb + *-ing*.
   Beispiele:
   You'll soon get used to living in the country.
   I can't get used to drinking tea all day.
8. In nächster Zeit heißt im Englischen *soon, some time soon* oder *in the near future*.

Übungsphase 1

1. *The actual cost was much higher than we had expected.*
2. *She takes an interest/is interested in the current events in Eastern Europe.*
3. *This church is a classic example of medieval architecture.*
4. *Many women want to change some typically male attitudes.*
5. *He has a rather feminine voice.*
6. *He looks very masculine in his new uniform.*
7. *The doctor told me to take three tablets before every meal.*
8. *He was only fourteen.*

Übungsphase 2

1. *We expect him to be back at 11 (o'clock).*
2. *They will have reached a decision by tomorrow.*
3. *Wait until/till I come.*
4. *I always diet in January. I always go on a diet in January.*
5. *As a Frenchman he is used to good food.*
6. *Southern Europeans, like (for example) Italians and Spaniards, use their hands more when talking. Southern Europeans, such as Italians and Spaniards, use their hands more when talking.*
7. *This year, everything is quite different.*
8. *I brush my teeth regularly.*

Übungsphase 3

1. *I have (got) a lot of work to do.*
2. *I like watching television/TV/telly, when I am tired.*
3. *Students should devote more time to reading.*
4. *Last year, she stopped going to discos.*
5. *No pupil likes homework.*
6. *My girl-friend/girlfriend is getting used to working less.*
7. *Many of my friends are going to study, for example/e.g./eg Janine, Sabine, Doris and Natascha.*
8. *My friend is getting married in the near future/some time soon/soon.*

Text 14

Fehlerkorrektur

1. *Lüneburg University* 2. *schoolchildren* 3. *marks* 4. *pressure* 5. *weigh heavily* 6. *imaginative children* 7. *criticism* 8. *enemy* 9. *suffer from stress* 10. *unjust* 11. *unjust to* 12. *final mark* 13. *on the one hand/on the other hand* 14. *frustration* 15. *treated unfairly* 16. *comparative figures* 17. *need not* 18. *regard negatively* 19. *favourite* 20. *subjects* 21. *physics*

Lernphase 1

1. Noten = *marks* („Schulnoten"), *note* („Musiknote", *notes/music* = Musiknoten), Kritik = *criticism*, Physik = *physics*.
   marks: The highest mark in the test was nine out of ten.
   notes/music: I still remember the first few notes of the tune. Give me my music and I'll play it for you.
   criticism: This decision has received a great deal of criticism.
   physics: Physics has made enormous progress in this century.
2. − −
3. Die korrekten Schreibungen lauten *schoolchildren, favourite subject* und *enemy*.
4. − −
5. *Weight* (v.) heißt im Deutschen „beschweren, belasten, schwerer machen", *weigh* heißt „wiegen, abwägen, lasten auf" (*on*).
6. *imaginable:* vorstellbar, denkbar, erdenklich
   imaginary: imaginär, (nur) eingebildet, frei erfunden
   imaginative: phantasievoll, einfallsreich
7. − −
8. − −
9. − −

Lernphase 2

1. *notes* = Musiknoten, Notizen, Geldnoten
   critic = Kritiker, Kritikerin
2. einerseits − andererseits = *on the one hand − on the other hand*
   on one side = auf der einen Seite (konkret): *John stood on one side of the ladder.*
   on the other side = auf der anderen Seite (konkret): *What does the leaflet say on the other side?*
3. − −
4. − −

5. – –
6. nicht müssen: *need not, not have (got) to*
   nicht brauchen: *need not, not have (got) to*
   nicht dürfen: **must not** (starkes Verbot), *may not* (Verbot), *not to be allowed/permitted to* (Verbot).
7. *esteem* = (hoch)achten, erachten: *The teacher was much loved and esteemed.*
   respect = respektieren, (be)achten: *I deeply respect her courage.*
   appreciate = (hoch)schätzen, würdigen, dankbar sein für: *His abilities were not appreciated in his job.*
   regard = ansehen, betrachten, achten: *I have always regarded her highly.*
8. Das Wort *topic* kann mit „Thema" (im Sinne von „Gegenstand einer Erörterung, Gesprächsgegenstand, Gesprächsgegenstand komplexer Natur") übersetzt werden. Das Wort *subject* (n.) kann „Thema" (im Sinne von „Gegenstand als abzuhandelnder oder behandelter Stoff, Thema mündlicher und schriftlicher Ausführungen"), „Staatsbürger"(bes. in einer Monarchie), „Fach", „(grammatisches) Subjekt", „Testperson" und „Anlaß zu" (*for*) heißen.
9. *physics:* Physik
   physique: Körperbau, Statur
   (*physic:* archaisch für „Medizin", „Mediziner", heute nicht mehr gebräuchlich)

Übungsphase 1

1. *I study at Keele University. I study at the University of Keele.*
2. *The hall was rapidly filling/rapidly filled with schoolchildren.*
3. *Nearly all the schoolchilden got a very good mark.*
4. *I cannot sing the high notes.*
5. *The pressure was unbearable.*
6. *His last argument weighed heavily.*
7. *She is a very imaginative student.*
8. *Many children develop fears of imaginary dangers.*
9. *We tried every imaginable means/every means imaginable, but we failed in the end.*

Übungsphase 2

1. *What did the London critics say about the new film?*
2. *She is one the most formidable enemies of the regime.*
3. *Everybody seems to suffer/to be suffering from too much stress.*
4. *The government's decisions are unjust to many women.*
5. *The final mark is always decisive.*
6. *On the one hand my job is well paid, on the other hand I have to work long hours.*
7. *Life is sometimes full of frustration.*
8. *I wonder why she treats him unfairly.*
9. *Have you (got) any comparative figures?*

Übungsphase 3

1. *We need not go to this meeting. We don't need to go to this meeting. We don't need go to this meeting. We don't have to go to this meeting. We haven't got to go to this meeting.*
2. *You must not cross this line.*
3. *I have always regarded him highly.*
4. *Who is your favourite actor?*
5. *I have chosen three subjects for my oral exam/examination.*
6. *Politics or religion are always interesting topics of conversation.*
7. *I hate physics.*
8. *His physique is magnificent.*

Text 15

Hinweis: Diejenigen Sätze, die im formellen BE verfaßt und mit dem AE identisch sind, werden nicht besonders gekennzeichnet.

Übungsphase 1

1. *Several countries co-operated to build a new plane. Several countries cooperated to build a new plane.*
2. *He must organize his life a bit better. He must organise his life a bit better.*
3. *This word's function is fairly limited. The function of this word is fairly limited.*
4. *Young people are sometimes much influenced by pop singers. Young people are sometimes very influenced by pop singers.*
5. *Non-verbal communication is often very difficult to interpret. Nonverbal communication is often very difficult to interpret.*
6. *You must avoid sweet foods, e.g. cake, ice cream and pudding. You must avoid sweet foods, eg cake, ice cream and pudding.* (bes. BE) *You must avoid sweet foods, for example cake, ice cream and pudding. You must avoid sweet foods, such as cake, ice cream and pudding.*
7. *I drive more slowly in snowy and icy conditions. I drive slower in snowy and icy conditions.*
8. *C. Ferguson? I don't know this person. Can you tell me where he lives? C. Ferguson? I don't know this person. Can you tell me where he or she lives?*

Übungsphase 2

1. *Her remark was just silly. Her remark was plain silly.* (infml.)
2. *They shook their heads when they heard the news. They shook their head when they heard the news.*
3. *The data is still being checked at the Census Office. The data are still being checked at the Census Office.*
4. *He looked upwards at the sky. He looked upward at the sky.* (bes. AE)
5. *He must have been very disturbed.*
6. *When one dines in the restaurant, a suit and tie are required. When dining in the restaurant, a suit and tie are required.*
7. *Try to stay calm. Try and stay calm.* (infml.)
8. *The members of the committee always try to keep an open mind and are ready/prepared to consider new ideas.*

Text 16

Fehlerkorrektur

1. *during a conversation*   2. *self-confident*   3. *you avoid looking*   4. *considered cold*   5. *friendly*   6. *we deviate from*   7. *for example/examples...*   8. *the question of space/personal space*   9. *interesting*   10. *fifty/sixty centimetres away from*   11. *aggressive*   12. *to touch each other*   13. *independent*   14. *independent of*   15. *cannot be studied independently*   16. *learners should become familiar with*

Lernphase 1

1. selbstbewußt = *self-confident, self-assured*, sympathisch = *pleasant, nice, likeable* (auch *likable*), *friendly*.
2. *self-conscious* = befangen, gehemmt, *sympathetic* = mitfühlend, teilnahmsvoll, verständnisvoll.
3. *during:* We go swimming every day during the summer. They lived abroad during the war.
   while: They arrived while we were having dinner. She got malaria while travelling in Africa.
4. – –
5. – –
6. – –
7. Die korrekten Schreibungen lauten *example, interesting, aggressive* und *independent*.

Lösungsteil · Text 16 113

Lernphase 2

1. – –
2. *room* = Zimmer, Saal, Platz (der eingenommen wird): *There is room for three on the back seat. There is room for doubt and suspicion.*
   space = Raum („begrenzter Raum, besonders zwischen zwei Punkten" oder „Zwischenraum"), Weltraum („der unendliche Raum" als wissenschaftlicher Begriff): *Keep some space between you and the car ahead. The satellite has been in space for a year.*
3. – –
4. *They touched themselves* (Reflexivpronomen) heißt „sie berührten sich selbst" (jede/r ihren/seinen eigenen Körper), während *they touched each other* (reziprokes Pronomen) im Deutschen mit „sie berührten sich gegenseitig" übersetzt werden kann.
5. – –
6. – –
7. *understand: I don't understand it. Can't you understand it?*
   check: We have checked the examples carefully. We read through the book to check for any mistakes.

Übungsphase 1

1. *One student fainted during the operation.*
2. *While the negotiations were still going on, the shooting started again.*
3. *Many actors are shy, but self-confident.*
4. *He felt self-conscious in this situation.*
5. *She avoided looking at him.*
6. *He was regarded as revengeful. He was considered (to be) revengeful. He was thought revengeful. He was counted (as) revengeful.*
7. *She is very pleasant/nice/likeable/likable/friendly.*
8. *I like him.*
9. *She was very sympathetic when she heard about the accident.*

Übungsphase 2

1. *He never deviates from his habits. For example, he always smokes after lunch.*
2. *We have not got enough space for all the new books.*
3. *I met a few interesting people on the beach.*
4. *He stood/was standing ten metres (away) from me.*
5. *He is a very aggressive person.*
6. *Do not touch me! Don't touch me!*
7. *They must learn to act independently.*
8. *India became independent of Britain in 1947.*
9. *I just do not understand why she did not check the tyre pressure. I just don't get why she didn't check the tyre pressure.* (infml.)

Korrekte Texte

Text 1
Mistakes

Teachers of English are always faced with the difficult problem of what to correct in their students' written and oral performance. Since the English language is constantly changing and since the notion of correctness and standard is never a hundred percent fixed, one must admit that the teachers' task is highly complicated. Furthermore, teachers are continually exposed to incorrect utterances from their students, so that ultimately teachers may have difficulty in recognizing mistakes. Thus, teachers will either overlook mistakes or mark items as incorrect which are actually correct. One cannot blame the students either, as it is of course typical of learners to make mistakes. Frankly speaking, it is high time that somebody published a comprehensive guide to help teachers correct texts properly.

Difficult areas in English where skills really do have to be developed are, for example, tense and aspect, proverbs, idioms and collocations. For example, can one talk about a "*strong smoker"? Does the proverb "*to carry owls to Athens" exist or should it be "to carry coals to Newcastle"? Can one say "I have been wanting to see this man for years"? And can an examination be "a piece of cake"? Hopefully, after working through this book, the reader might feel more competent to deal with such questions.

Text 2
Sponsored Students

Recently I read an article about a new phenomenon in British universities – the sponsored student. After leaving his grammar school, John D. received a grant from a well-known firm of estate agents enabling him to go to university. He was quoted as saying that a sponsored student certainly needs to be self-assured, as he must be prepared to display information about his sponsoring firm in the form of slogans on T-shirts or other articles of clothing. John is good at geography and is studying property changes in England over the last 50 years. But he denied that being sponsored has affected his studies in any way, although most of his essays do end with a recommendation of his sponsoring firm. As the reader may have guessed, all that John wants to do after taking his exams is to go to work for a certain firm of estate agents.

Text 3
Violence on TV

For reasons of principle, it would of course be preferable if people watched less TV than they do. But there is such a large choice of programmes available that it is not surprising that the ordinary man in the street spends too much time at home, remote control in hand and eyes glued to the screen. And, of course, the choice of viewing material has been greatly increased by the availability of video films. One of the most disturbing developments is the increase in the sales of video "nasties" – video films containing a particularly high proportion of sex and violence. A recent parliamentary report showed that these videos are especially harmful to children, who do not notice that there is a difference between life on the screen and real life. Young sensitive children often have nightmares and display increased aggression after watching such videos. We have even reached a stage where older children challenge younger ones to watch videos which are really gruesome. It is feared that this trend will continue unless the government forms a committee to take steps to have these video "nasties" banned.

Text 4

The Open University

In 1971, an educational experiment began in Milton Keynes, England, which has affected the lives of thousands of people in Britain. This was the start of the Open University. The aim of the Open University is to provide degree courses (including doctorates) for anyone, regardless of previous qualifications. The Open University devotes itself almost entirely to teaching by correspondence, although radio and television broadcasts are also part of the course. The university authorities work closely with the BBC in planning broadcasts. In fact, the TV screen is in some ways superior to a lecture-room, allowing close-ups of experiments and providing glimpses of work in research centres, which might not otherwise be available to students. Students receive weekly correspondence of programmed explanations and exercises and also book-lists complete with the names and addresses of bookshops where the books can be bought. The books are cheap, because publishers can mass-produce copies for the Open University which usually sell well and which sometimes become best sellers. Science students receive material at home free of charge for carrying out experiments.

Personal contact between students and lecturers is established during summer courses lasting about two weeks at a normal university or college. Each student also has the opportunity all year round to visit a local study centre, of which there are about two hundred all over the country. Here, he or she can work with other students under the guidance of a tutor. With this type of organization, the Open University needs few buildings and little apparatus as it uses existing facilities in other universities during the summer vacation.

The Open University has consistently adhered to the principle of offering further education to people of all ages and walks of life, and they have eagerly grasped this opportunity. They range from workers who left school at sixteen to professional people working for higher qualifications such as a BA, an MA or even a PhD. And now, as it nears its twentieth anniversary, the standards and popularity of this institution appear to be as high as ever.

Text 5
Keeping Out the Sun

These days, the "greenhouse effect" is a phrase with which we are all familiar. It is a result of the discharge of gases (from many and varied processes) which are causing the earth's temperature to rise. This would, in its turn, cause a world-wide change in climate resulting in a huge man-made catastrophe.

A Swiss scientist has used his imagination and come up with a plan, bordering on science fiction, to avoid the disruption of the climate caused by the greenhouse effect. His plan is to place a series of mirrors in a special orbit to cast a shadow over part of the earth. These mirrors would reflect a proportion of sunshine back into space. His theory is that the mirrors would compensate for a 2.5°C rise in the average global temperature, by reducing the amount of incoming sunshine by about 3.5 percent. This device would counteract greenhouse warming successfully. It is comparable to a sunshade of huge mirrors.

He claims that the scheme would cost the equivalent of the world's annual military expenditure, about four hundred billion pounds. But, even using the latest lightweight materials to build the mirror satellites, it is estimated that it would take twenty years to build them. Some people are of course likely to be sceptical – however, this is after all a high-tech solution to a problem requiring drastic measures.

Text 6 (Vgl. S. 29)

Text 7
Traffic Jams – A Thing of the Past?

Los Angeles boasts the three busiest roads in the world and consequently the worst traffic jams. Planners reckon that in the next twenty years the number of daily car journeys will rise by forty per cent, and the average speed on freeways will be halved. There are many possible solutions to this problem. The car lobby would like money to be spent on new roads. Local authorities in Los Angeles would like to repeat the experience of the 1984 Olympics, when an increase in the number of bus journeys and staggered journey times kept Los Angeles free of traffic jams for two weeks. Rail enthusiasts are pinning their hopes on a projected new light railway. But the most promising solutions rely on new technology – research is being done in three main fields.

Firstly, streets are being equipped with road sensors which monitor traffic flow and are linked to central computers. These instantly adjust traffic lights to control the traffic. A second system aims at placing computers in cars, giving drivers up to the minute advice on road conditions ahead (for example accidents or jams), thus enabling them to take alternative routes. Cars could also be fitted with radar which relays signals to a computer situated in the car and prevents collisions by automatically braking the car. Eventually, one of the safety measures might include a device whereby a driver who

has had a couple of drinks too many will automatically be prevented from driving his or her car.
The overall aim is to automate driving – similar to the way modern aeroplanes function – taking much of the control of driving out of the driver's hands. A further problem may of course be providing parking spaces for all the extra cars which this system allows to use the city streets!

Text 8
What Weather!

Humans first set foot in Britain more than half a million years ago. The surprising fact is that ancient Britons appear to have stayed on only when the weather was inclement. Britons apparently clung to their shores just so that they could go on complaining about the weather! Archaeologists have noticed that when the climate became warm and food in the form of bison and mammoth roamed the land, ancient Britons seem to have vanished – as evidenced by a stark lack of remains from these times.
The climate has regularly swung between periods of very hot and cold weather, from ice ages to heatwaves. In between these extremes, the country was covered with tundra and wet mists. We would find this rather inhospitable as we are currently going through a warm period and are used to living in much better conditions. We also learn from archaeologists that Britain was nevertheless inhabitable with its tundra and mist and that ancient Britons seem to have thrived on it, since nearly all ancient sites in Britain date from these cool periods. Obviously, such weather represented no threat to ancient Britons. For example, a huge mammoth graveyard uncovered near Ipswich indicates a spot where dozens of animals died. Bearing in mind that mammoths roamed the land in warm conditions, they should have provided food for scavenging humans, but flints – the only sure proof of ancient humans' presence – are totally missing. In so far as our information about this period is correct, there is strong reason to believe that there were simply no humans around to take advantage of this opportunity.
Various explanations, most of them not very satisfactory, have been put forward, but the only certain conclusion seems to be that ancient Britons appear to have had a strange urge to hang about in the cold and rain!

Text 9 (Vgl. S. 43)

Text 10
Environmental Pollution Poses No Threat

If ecological experts are to be believed, the future of the planet Earth looks grim indeed. We are slowly extinguishing the natural environment with loops of concrete across the countryside carrying cars belching toxic fumes, with concrete tower blocks excluding all sunlight, and with factories and power stations doing their best to choke us to death. And we are poisoning the soil, rivers, the air – the list is inexhaustible. We can already imagine what the earth will look like if we do not put a stop to pollution immediately.

Faced with this gloomy prospect, the efforts of societies to save a single tree, or restore an ancient building seem futile and irrelevant. So why keep on worrying about environmentally friendly behaviour? Why try to put off the inevitable? Picking up a sweet paper to put it in a litter bin or switching off the car engine at traffic lights seems comically absurd.

If we consider the fact that earlier creatures coped with changes in the environment and adapted – why can't we? The optimist in us stirs. All the old guilty feelings associated with, for example, not doing enough exercise to keep ourselves fit, fall away. No more jogging, walking, or press-ups. The "New Human Beings" are pear-shaped, soft and self-complacent. They can eat fattening foods without any fears. The slavery of cleaning teeth is over. Nourished on the sugary delights of the supermarket in soft and liquid form, they will no longer need their meat-eating teeth, which will simply fall out. They will no longer be allergic to bad air, but will be able to inhale poisonous fumes, knowing they are evolving lungs to flourish on them. They can take up lodgings underneath the flight path to an airport, knowing that their ear-drums are evolving to cope with the thunder of landing planes.

Their families will learn to picnic in underpasses and on fly-overs (fields will have disappeared), eating pre-packed food to the roar of traffic and amplified music. As for human language, its loss will not be too tragic, since post-verbal communication will be in the form of grunts and grimaces. So, prepare for mutation! It's later than you think.

Text 11

The Modern European

With the approach of 1992, when customs barriers will fall throughout Europe, great changes are to be expected. One of these will concern people's attitudes towards language learning. At the moment, there is a proliferation of language learning in Europe. Ideally speaking, "the Eurocrat of 1992" will be like a Swiss – speaking at least three languages, ie his or her mother tongue, English and one other foreign language.

Bowing to feelings of national pride, the EC can boast no fewer than nine official languages. But to limit its cost, the EC conducts most ot its business in three working languages: English, French and German. And in practice, English is the language of choice in commerce, science, technology, advertising and public relations.

However there are compelling reasons for executives and salespeople to be multilingual. For example, in a business deal, a German speaking English has a distinct advantage over an Englishman who does not speak German. Faced with ever

increasing economic competition within the EC, even the British are becoming convinced of the fact that foreign languages are vital to them. As a result, language schools are opening up all over Britain, and in Europe as a whole, a well-known language school has doubled its teaching load in the last five years.
The British have been notorious for their lack of interest in foreign languages, but now the advent of 1992 along with the construction of the Channel Tunnel seem to be eroding Britain's insularity. Britain can no longer afford to lose touch with this development and changes in the school curriculum will now make it compulsory for British schoolchildren to learn at least one foreign language up to the age of sixteen. In other words, the British are bowing to the inevitable.
A further question is how Europe's languages will fare after 1992. Some experts foresee the day when a Europeanised form of English – perhaps we could call it "Eurolish" – will be the common language in Europe. The smaller languages would fall into disuse. Other linguists see a danger of a regionalisation of languages and cultures, with some languages being restricted to rural areas. Yet others maintain that by retaining nine official languages, the EC may have stopped the decline of smaller languages.

Text 12

Crime Does Pay!

Even Hercule Poirot, that master of logical deduction, might be surprised at the continuing success of his creator, Agatha Christie. She remains the leader in tables of sales and royalties earned. Some people claim she has even outsold William Shakespeare himself. Agatha Christie's novels have become an English institution. She wrote eighty-four altogether, in addition to nineteen plays and four non-fictional books. 1990 is the centenary of her birth and will no doubt provide us with a whole year of commemoration and even larger sales.
Agatha Christie was quite a character herself, since her own life was something of a riddle. She was born in Devon. Her American father died when she was a child and her mother brought her up in true Edwardian style. It was the break-up of Agatha Christie's first marriage to Archibald Christie in 1928, which made her a household name. After learning of her husband's involvement with another woman, she disappeared from home, causing a nationwide police search. She was found in a hotel in Harrogate registered under the name of her husband's lover. The family claimed that she had suffered from amnesia, but the riddle has never been satisfactorily solved. Two years later, she married Max Mallowan, who was an archaeologist. The couple travelled to Istanbul, Egypt and Baghdad, which provided the setting for many of her plots.
Agatha Christie died in 1976, leaving Agatha Christie Ltd. to her family, and her grandson now runs the firm.
An interesting question remains – how has Agatha Christie managed to retain her popularity for so long? Her literary agent claims that the presentation of her works on the film screen and on television has led to a revival. The film "Murder on the Orient

Express" had already established the potential of the stories as vehicles for nostalgia. He also believes that the style and the elegant atmosphere of the good old days in her books appealed to the public of the seventies and eighties. The West End play "The Mousetrap" certainly testifies to her continuing popularity – it is the longest-running play in history, its debut having been in 1952.

Text 13

Young People in the Eighties

The results of a survey of young people's behaviour carried out in Britain have been summarised in a recent report entitled "Young People in 1987" and published by the Health Education Authority. It reveals that the differences between the sexes are greater than any changes in teenage behaviour over the past few years. A striking example of different male and female behaviour concerns drugs and pain killers. The survey shows that one of the most worrying features was that girls apparently use far more pain killers than boys. Boys, however, are more involved in taking illegal drugs, although total numbers are very low. Less than one percent of young people between fourteen and sixteen had taken heroin. Cannabis is still the most widely-used drug among teenagers.

As society expects girls to be slim, it is not surprising that girls are much more concerned about weight problems than boys. By the time they are fifteen, two-thirds have dieted at least once. Fewer boys try to slim and the trend decreases with age. Boys also consume more "junk food" like fizzy drinks and chocolate, while girls prefer fruit. Strangely enough, the most popular food or drink overall was fruit juice.

Further results show that the attitudes of boys and girls towards grooming and cleanliness are quite different. Girls bath and brush their teeth more regularly than boys. Other differences can be seen in attitudes towards work and leisure activities. Boys spend a lot of time watching television, playing computer and slot machine games and "hanging about" in the street, whereas girls devote their time to doing work for school or going to parties and discos. Girls of all ages do more homework than boys. However, the number of teenagers who have stopped doing homework altogether increases between the ages of eleven and sixteen.

Girls, in contrast to boys, develop certain adult habits rather quickly, e.g. girls get used to drinking alcohol and smoking early in life and are more likely to have a steady boyfriend by the age of fifteen. Despite certain worrying factors, the report ends on an optimistic note by showing that smoking and drinking among teenagers has decreased overall and only a tiny fraction is involved in drug-taking. There is hope that this positive trend will continue in the near future.

Text 14
School in West Germany

A group of professors from Lüneburg University in the Federal Republic of Germany recently revealed some of the results of a survey carried out among German schoolchildren. The children were asked to give their opinions about teachers, syllabuses and marks in the form of written essays. Seven thousand in Lower Saxony and Bavaria were involved in the survey as well as a comparative group of five thousand pupils from Sweden, England and the United States.

The results of this survey indicate that marks, school reports and competitive pressure to succeed weigh heavily on German pupils – the more so the older they are. Some of the phrases used by pupils in their essays to describe school were "a prison", "a cage", "an institution which swallows up imaginative children and turns them out at the other end all in the same uniform grey which characterises the school building".

The main criticism of the syllabus was that it was too theoretical. And a large number of pupils see tests and the resultant marks as their "greatest enemy". In the eleventh class, 55.5 % of pupils suffer from stress associated with pressure to succeed. 42.6% of all grammar school pupils criticise the marking system. Marks seem to be especially unjust to pupils, since class tests are usually not evaluated objectively. In addition, oral work, which plays a dominant role in determining the final mark, is also assessed subjectively by the teacher. On the one hand, this system encourages pupils to do everything "to get in" with the teacher, on the other hand it creates frustration, mistrust and even disgust in quite a number of young people, who feel that they are treated unfairly. Comparative figures from abroad show that marks at least need not be such a source of dissatisfaction. In West Germany, 27.8% of the pupils regard marks negatively, whereas in Sweden this figure is 10.6%, in the United States 4.3% and in England only 2.1%.

The motivation experienced by German pupils is correspondingly low. Only 12.7% of secondary school pupils and 18.8% of those at grammar schools actually like going to school. It is certainly symptomatic that sport, art and music are pupils' favourite subjects with physics and chemistry at the bottom of the list.

Text 15 (Vgl. S. 71)

Text 16
Communicating II

Another important source of information about a person is his or her face and especially the eyes. If you look at another person's eyes a lot during a conversation, people will think that you are open, friendly and self-confident. If you avoid looking at the other person, you will be considered cold and defensive. Southern Europeans look at each other more than Northern Europeans. Thus Italians might find English people serious and cold, whereas English people may find Italians friendly – neither of which may be the case.

In an ordinary conversation, we spend about a third of the time looking at each other, and this eye contact follows a certain pattern. If we deviate from this pattern, it will communicate a special meaning. For example, if we are nervous of someone, we do not look at them much. We stare at someone when we are angry or anxious, and longer eye contact than normal suggests that we are attracted to the other person.

Another aspect of communication concerns the question of space. People usually like to mark their personal space. For example, on the beach you may spread out a towel, or in a train you often put a bag or a coat on the seat next to you.

An interesting aspect of this is the physical distance people put between one another when talking. An American psychologist has found that when conversing, American males stand approximately fifty centimetres away from another man, and sixty centimetres away from a woman. If they are closer than this, they are either very aggressive or very friendly. However, in South America or the Middle East, people stand much closer than this when conversing and are much more likely to touch each other than the British for example.

These few examples show that language behaviour cannot be studied independently of people's socio-cultural backgrounds. Consequently, language learners should become familiar with these socio-cultural conventions. Knowing that these conventions exist can help to avoid misunderstandings in communication.

ANHANG

Zur Problematik der Fehleridentifizierung: Korrektheit im modernen Englischen

Als Abschluß des Buches soll hier aus praktischer Sicht eine Zusammenfassung zum Problem der Norm und des Sprachgebrauchs in Hinblick auf die Fehleridentifizierung geliefert werden. Die Ausführungen basieren hauptsächlich auf den Forschungsarbeiten von Lakoff, Legenhausen, Quirk, Greenbaum, Leech, Svartvik, Mittins und auf eigenen Publikationen. Im Zusammenhang mit dem Problem der grammatischen Akzeptabilität sei vor allem auf Lakoffs und Legenhausens Überlegungen verwiesen, welche in Teilen übernommen wurden. Eine kurze Bibliographie dient dazu, eine Einführung in die Norm- und Sprachgebrauchsproblematik zu geben. Schließlich werden neuere Handbücher empfohlen, welche bei der Korrekturarbeit eine konkrete Hilfe sein können.

Folgende Punkte sollten beim Problem der Fehleridentifizierung im modernen Englischen bedacht werden:

1. Bei allen Korrekturen im Fremdsprachenunterricht zeigt sich, daß unterschiedliche Bewertungen von schriftlichen Leistungen zunächst deshalb zustandekommen, weil Muttersprachler und Nicht-Muttersprachler nicht in gleicher Weise in der Sprache kompetent sind. Außerdem können unterschiedliche Korrekturerfahrungen, Korrekturtraditionen, Zeitdruck und manchmal auch mangelnde Sorgfalt eine Rolle spielen.

2. Wie jede lebende Sprache wandelt sich das Englische ständig. Es ist daher natürlich, daß Korrektheitsvorstellungen sowie Ansichten zu *usage*-Fragen einem dauernden Wechsel unterliegen: Korrektheit richtet sich nach dem Sprachgebrauch, und aller Sprachgebrauch ist relativ.

3. Die Korrektheitsproblematik kann heutzutage in sehr vielen Fällen nicht mehr auf eine simple Ja-oder-nein-Entscheidung reduziert werden (Ausnahme: Orthographiefehler, teilweise auch Zeichensetzungsfehler). Empirische Untersuchungen zur Sprachgebrauchsproblematik bestätigen, daß gebildete Sprecher des Englischen nicht alle sprachlichen Äußerungen, die ihnen zur Bewertung vorlagen, als entweder korrekt oder inkorrekt bezeichneten, sondern es bestand darüber hinaus die Notwendigkeit, weitere Abstufungen vorzunehmen. Die Bestimmung dessen, was im Englischen als sprachliche Abweichung zu gelten hat, ganz unabhängig davon, wer diese Bestimmung vornimmt, erweist sich als ein sehr schwieriges Unterfangen. Hier sind vor allem sprachinhärente Schwierigkeiten zu nennen, da der Begriff der Standardsprache ein theoretisches Konstrukt ist, welches nur in gewissem Maße empirisch verifizierbar ist. *Standard English* ist zudem nicht monolithisch, sondern muß diastratisch (sozial), diaphasisch (stilistisch), diachron (historisch) und diatopisch (regio-

nal) gesehen werden. Damit ist die Standardsprache in ein mehrdimensionales Varietätenkontinuum eingebunden. Für die Praxis bedeutet das folgendes:

3.1. In einem erweiterten Korrektheitsbegriff, der die Abstufungen in *acceptable usage, divided usage, ill-established usage, dubious usage* und *unacceptable usage* vornimmt, muß dem *divided usage* von den Korrektoren eine besondere Aufmerksamkeit geschenkt werden, da dieser aus linguistischer Sicht Teil der korrekten Standardsprache geworden ist. Dieser Ansatz ist in der *Comprehensive Grammar of the English Language* konsequent verwirklicht. Die verschiedenen Akzeptabilitätsstufen werden wie folgt gekennzeichnet: *unacceptable, ?**tending to unacceptability,* ? *native speakers unsure about acceptability,* (*) bzw. (?) *native speakers differ in their reactions.*

3.2. Alle nationalen Standardvarietäten des Englischen (besonders das BE und AE) und auch die funktionalen Varietäten von *very formal* bis *very informal* in der gesprochenen und geschriebenen Sprache müssen als **korrekt** eingestuft werden. Das Vergreifen im Stil oder das Mischen von AE und BE ist also nicht als Verstoß im Sinne von sprachlicher Inkorrektheit (*unacceptable usage*), sondern als Stilfehler (*inappropriate language*) zu werten, der konsequenterweise seinen Niederschlag in der Stilnote findet.

3.3. Man kann davon ausgehen, daß sehr viele sprachliche Erscheinungen eine Grauzone aufweisen, in welcher die Intuitionen der Muttersprachler verschwommen, uneindeutig oder sogar auch widersprüchlich werden. Diese Tatsache ist erst in den letzten 15 Jahren stärker in den Mittelpunkt der linguistischen Forschung gerückt und wurde zunächst unter dem Begriff der *fuzzy grammar* diskutiert.

Grammatische Uneindeutigkeit wird im Rahmen der *fuzzy grammar* (heute *cognitive grammar*) nicht mehr als periphere Erscheinung gedeutet, sondern muß als wichtiges Explikandum von Sprache überhaupt gewertet werden. G. Lakoff schrieb bereits 1973:

„a) Rules of grammar do not simply apply or fail to apply, rather they apply to a degree.

b) Grammatical elements are not simply members or nonmembers of grammatical categories, rather they are members to a degree."

Beispiele sind u.a. Adjektive wie *young, ablaze, asleep, old, perfect* (*attributive only, predicative only, premodification with very, comparison*), Kollokationen mit *utterly*, der Gebrauch von Präpositionen (*typical of/? for, characteristic of/? for, example of/? for*) oder die unterschiedliche Behandlung der Übereinstimmung zwischen Nomen und Verb (*grammatical concord, notional concord* und *concord of proximity*).

Nur mit einem so radikal veränderten Beschreibungsansatz wird erklärbar, warum auch *native speakers* mit vergleichbarer Spracherfahrung ein erstaunliches Maß an interindividueller Variation bei Akzeptabilitätsbefragungen aufweisen.

4. Konsequenzen für die Korrektur
Als praktische Konsequenz aus dem Gesagten kann folgende Empfehlung an die korrigierenden Lehrerinnen und Lehrer ausgesprochen werden:
Als Maßstab für die Korrektur können nur Standardgrammatiken und Standardwörterbücher herangezogen werden,
a) welche den neuesten, empirisch ermittelten Sprachstand der *educated native speakers* widerspiegeln,
b) welche dem gewandelten Korrektheitsbegriff Rechnung tragen,
c) die zumindest Kennzeichnungen in Hinblick auf die Sprachebene (formell – informell), auf das Medium (geschrieben – gesprochen), auf die Häufigkeit (selten – häufig), auf den aktuellen Grad der Gebräuchlichkeit (archaisch, veraltet, altmodisch), auf den Texttyp (biblisch, literarisch, medizinisch, technisch) sowie auf die nationalen und sozioregionalen Varietäten enthalten und
d) die schließlich aufgrund empirischer Sprachdaten und aufgrund von Akzeptabilitätsbefragungen der *educated native speakers* explizit zu einzelnen Sprachgebrauchserscheinungen (*usage notes*) Stellung nehmen.

Diese Ansprüche erfüllen im allgemeinen weder die in großer Zahl erschienenen *usage guides* noch von Nichtmuttersprachlern verfaßte Handbücher, sondern in erster Linie von Muttersprachlern erstellte Standardgrammatiken und Standardwörterbücher. Folgende herausragende Werke sind in dieser Hinsicht zu nennen:

Comprehensive Grammar of the English Language (1985). London: Longman, Hgg. Quirk, Greenbaum, Leech und Svartvik

COBUILD English Language Dictionary (1987). London: Collins

Dictionary of Contemporary English (1987). London: Longman

Oxford Advanced Learner's Dictionary (1989). London: Oxford University Press

Student's Dictionary of Collocations (1989). Berlin: Cornelsen, Hgg. Benson, Benson und Ilson.

Weitere Hilfsmittel für die Korrektur sind u.a. auch noch folgende Werke:

Lamprecht (1986) *Grammatik der englischen Sprache*. Berlin: Cornelsen

Ungerer/Meier/Schäfer/Lechler (1985) *A Grammar of Present-Day English*. Stuttgart: Klett

Swan (1980/88) *Practical English Usage*. London: Oxford University Press.

5. Insgesamt stellt die Korrektur von Englischarbeiten sehr große Anforderungen an die Lehrerinnen und Lehrer. Es wäre deshalb wünschenswert, wenn diese Arbeit von gegenseitiger Toleranz und mit viel kollegialem Verständnis getragen würde.

Bibliographie

Dretzke, B. (1981) „Sprachgebrauch, Korrektheit und Fehleridentifizierung aus praktischer Sicht", in: Kunsmann, P./O. Kuhn, Hgg. (1981) *Weltsprache Englisch in Forschung und Lehre, Festschrift für Kurt Wächtler*. Berlin: Erich Schmidt Verlag, 272–287

Dretzke, B. (1989) "Modern British English Usage – Problems for Non-Natives and Natives", *Zielsprache Englisch*, 1 (1989), 4–9

Dretzke, B. (1992) „Neuerungen in der englischen Sprache – Divided Usages", *Fremdsprachenunterricht*, 2 (1992), 90–93

Lakoff, G. (1973) "Fuzzy grammar and the performance/competence terminology game", *Papers from the 9th Regional Meeting of the Chicago Linguistic Society*. Chicago: Chicago University Press, 271–291

Legenhausen, L. (1988) „Fehler-*Fuzziness* und Bewertungsvarianz", in: Finkenstaedt, Th./F.-R. Weller, Hgg. (1988) *Schrittweise zur Validität*. Augsburg: I & I-Schriften, 211–233

Legenhausen, L. (1989) „*Grammatical Fuzziness* im Englischen", *Arbeiten aus Anglistik und Amerikanistik*, Band 14, Heft 1 (1989), 73–88

Mittins, W.H. (1988) *English: Not the Naming of Parts*. Sheffield: NATE

Mittins, W.H./M. Salu/M. Edminson/S. Coyne (1970) *Attitudes to English Usage*. London: Oxford University Press